THE SOUL OF THE CONGREGATION

THE SOUL OF THE CONGREGATION
AN INVITATION TO CONGREGATIONAL
REFLECTION

Thomas Edward Frank

Abingdon Press
Nashville

THE SOUL OF THE CONGREGATION
AN INVITATION TO CONGREGATIONAL REFLECTION

This book is printed on acid-free, elemental-chlorine-free paper.

Library of Congress Cataloging-in-Publication Data

Frank, Thomas Edward.
  The soul of the congregation: an invitation to Congregational Reflection / Thomas Edward Frank.
    p. cm.
  Includes bibliographical references and index.
  ISBN 0-687-08717-1 (alk. paper)
  1. Church. 2. Mission of the church. I. Title.

BV601.7 .F73 2000
250—dc21   99-056255

00 01 02 03 04 05 06 07 08 09 — 10 9 8 7 6 5 4 3 2 1

MANUFACTURED IN THE UNITED STATES OF AMERICA

To
Ken Gottman
and
Bob Reber

Contents

Preface

After church on Sundays, after coffee hour, after the congregation was gone and no one remained but Max—the custodian—and me, I would sometimes wander back into the sanctuary and walk the aisles. By then I had hung my robe and stole in the office, and the paraments had been folded and put away. The Webbs would be taking the altar flowers to old Mrs. Crenshaw. A few petals would be scattered on the platform steps, and I would bend to pick up an Easter lily order form that had fallen from a bulletin. I could still detect the faintest hint of sweet blossoms, the scent hovering in the close air with the waxy smoke of extinguished candles and the remains of perfume and cologne. The organ and piano were silent now, my pulpit phrases long gone. The boards creaked loudly under my feet. The sun had already moved around to shine full through the south windows illuminating brilliant colors that most parishioners never saw.

And I would think, who are we now? Where are we now? Who is this congregation, anyway? When we were assembled in that place, I always thought I knew. The loyals would be in their proper pews. The announcements would point to numerous activities. The routine of liturgy would convince me that we were a group of people that knew what we were doing.

But in the solitude of the sanctuary my questions only grew. What is a congregation, anyway? Who are these people and why do they keep coming here? Can a corporate group of wildly diverse individuals with all their idiosyncrasies really form a coherent identity and purpose out of mere weekly assemblies? If they did, it would be a miracle. So how is it that this miracle happens so often?

The longer I pastored congregations, the more bluntly my ignorance confronted me. I had college and seminary degrees, even doctoral work behind me, but I did not know what any good country preacher, rooted in the land and community, knows by instinct (but may not know he or she knows). I had never considered the congregation as a corporate group that stays together over time, that grows up and old together, that develops its own distinctive character.

I had a lot of pieces of perspective, but the fragments did not make a whole. My foundations in Bible, church history, and theology were strong; I knew or could quickly resurrect most of the principal theories and themes. Best of all I had learned methods for continuing to grow in my knowledge of Christian tradition; this was certainly to the good. I had sound training in various pastoral skills and practiced them avidly. My preaching was growing in depth; I was getting better at organizing sensible worship services; my counseling seemed to help people; I was becoming more patient and receptive in my hospital and home visits. I thought I was a whiz at planning church meetings, and prided myself on tight agendas and clear proposals. In fact, I had lots of program ideas for my congregations. I thrived on learning more about the community, networking with other institutions, planning ecumenical activities, and figuring out how my congregations could better respond to neighborhood needs. I was always on the go.

This fragmented and frantic life was exhilarating much of the time. Sometimes it was exhausting. It could be crushingly lonely. For a long time I assumed that all these diverse activities could make sense only in me—that it was my integrity alone that could unify them. Endless hours of introspection brought me some degree of centeredness, as I weighed all the things I was doing and rationalized their place in my ministry. But I still felt scattered and unaffirmed in my work.

Meanwhile, I was puzzled by a dimension of pastoring congregations that I had never considered before. The same people kept turning up in my ministry, whichever discrete pastoral skill I was practicing at the moment. I would have lunch with Pete to plan the finance committee meeting one day, visit his home to console him about the divorce of his fair-haired son another day, and scan his face as I preached about Lazarus and social justice on the Sabbath. I would drop by Elizabeth's home for the circle meeting on Tuesday and visit there with Frances and Pauline and the rest of the women now in their eighties. Then I would see them again at my Bible study on Thursday and sit with them at fellowship dinner on Sunday. I began to realize that pastoral ministry is a profoundly personal profession, and that nothing could be more important than being the same person in all these settings. That made my integrity and centeredness all the more important.

But I also began to realize that these people had been together for a while, some of them for a long time, and that I was just passing through. I began to wonder what centered them as a corporate group, and what held them there. I found myself reconsidering my proposals to sell the old parlor furniture given by the Gilchrist family and to try a second Sunday morning service. First I needed to understand these people better as an enduring community of faith.

Time and distance have brought me some further wisdom about the congregations I served. I know now that the integrity of my pastoral work depended on me, to be sure, but that it was also shaped by the corporate character of the people I pastored. The congregation itself in its persistent gathering and working was the centering force in my scattered efforts. The congregation itself gave me the compass points for my journey in ministry.

One further insight has followed from this: I realize now that for all my ideas and skills eagerly put into practice, the truth is I had no theology of the congregation. I had various notions of what to preach; these I advocated fervently. I was sure of the biblical mandates to help the helpless; these I pushed into action. But I had no sure ground for understanding the congregation itself as ecclesia, a people of God called together and gifted for ministry in a particular place, a people who in assembling week by week weave a fabric of stories and symbols and actions and memories and hopes that endures from generation to generation, and that becomes a finite local culture in which God's promised reign is embodied, if only in moments and glimpses.

I think it may have been the scandal of this particularity that made me stumble and miss what was right in front of me. It seemed brazen and heretical to claim much about God's presence in the finitude of a grandiose old neo-Gothic building filled with people who like me were narrowly focused on their own needs and interests. I grew to loathe sweeping pulpit pronouncements that "God is here this morning." I wondered who we thought we were to be addressing God so confidently. Yet out of the materials of tuneless hymns, rushed coffee conversations, endless meetings and poorly attended Bible studies, God still shaped a people, and for that I can only express wonder and thanks.

These letters and reflections will explore how to

learn more of that congregational culture and some ways to think about it theologically. I am aware what a gift it is for me to enjoy enough respite from the rush of pastoring to be able to ponder what I have experienced. I have always had difficulty seeing the culture in which I was immersed, or considering its meaning.

Yet what I propose in my letters and reflections is not arcane knowledge available only to specialists. Reaching for a deeper understanding of congregations is simply a more deliberate practice of an art in which people called to ministry are already gifted to one degree or another. It is an art of seeing, listening, paying attention, and spinning webs of connection with experiences, memories, traditions, and ideas that have gone before. It is an art of discernment that can only be honed in the practice of it. It is, in short, a practice of poetics that gifts those who pursue it with insight and imagination. And so as I write I am especially grateful to the congregations who taught me to look and listen, to discern, and within the bounds of their limitations and mine, their gifts and mine, to be a pastor.

I could never have written this book without all the churches and institutions in which I've been privileged to live and work. I want first to name the congregations in which my own arts of ministry were developed, and in which I first became aware of the culture and poetics of congregational life. These include the church of my childhood, Grace United Methodist Church in St. Louis, as well as the churches in which I served as a pastor—Missouri United Methodist Church in Columbia and University United Methodist Church in University City, Missouri. The people of these churches, as well as

St. Paul United Methodist Church in Atlanta, have been a profound influence on my life and work, by word and example. I am grateful to them and wish I had room to record even more about them and their collective life as congregations.

I am thankful for the many churches with whom I have had the opportunity to consult, or who have invited me in to study and learn from them. Mayflower Congregational Church in Grand Rapids, Michigan, is prominent among them, and the letters in this book are addressed to their pastor and my friend and colleague Ken Gottman. Many others are in the Atlanta area, of which I mention particularly the three congregations that welcomed our research team from Candler a few years ago: St. Luke's Episcopal Church, Big Bethel African Methodist Episcopal Church, and Oakhurst Baptist Church.

I can't imagine a more stimulating group of colleagues or an institution more supportive of research and writing on the church than Candler School of Theology. I've had the particular privilege of working together with James W. Fowler on a project exploring the relationship of congregations and public life. He assessed his learnings from that project in his book *Weaving the New Creation: Stages of Faith and the Public Church* (HarperSanFrancisco, 1991), and we wrote an unpublished paper together, "Living Toward Public Church: Three Congregations," on which I have drawn heavily here. The graduate student research team of Andrew Grant, Kurt Keljo, George Kloster, Pamela Moeller, Joseph Reiff, Fred Smith, Scott Thumma, Cheryl Walker, and Michael Wyatt contributed immensely to our common work, and it has been exciting to see each of them move on into their own professional work continuing their distinct contributions to scholarship and ministry.

That project grew into an even broader program of congregational studies that I directed involving six other colleagues and twenty other congregations. These scholars included Pamela Couture, Charles Foster, Robert Franklin, Gail O'Day, Sally Purvis, and Don Saliers, who went on to publish various articles and books from their studies here. I wrote an article for the journal *Theological Education* that distilled many of our collective learnings, "Congregations and Theological Education and Research." But that is only one effort to say all that I learned from them, and from Rebecca Chopp who consulted with us regularly.

These research programs were supported not only by Candler and its administration, in particular Dean James Waits and Dean Kevin LaGree, but by the Pew Charitable Trusts and the Lilly Endowment. I want to thank especially James P. Wind, then with Lilly and now President of The Alban Institute, for his support of our work and for his own insights into congregational studies from which I have learned so much.

I'm also thankful to Diane Bonds, Rebecca Chopp, Susan Henry-Crowe, Steven Kraftchick, Brian Mahan, Carol Newsom, and Don Saliers for very helpful reading of the manuscript, conversations, and suggestions along the way. I am especially grateful to Gail O'Day for her generous time and effort in the editing of an unruly manuscript, and for her constant encouragement in the final stages toward publication.

Who can possibly name all the conversations that provoke imagination and make one think in new ways? The words and images flow together in a refreshing stream from one encounter to the next. I benefited greatly from participating in James Gustafson's last interdisciplinary seminar for faculty at Emory, which he conducted with Walter Reed in Spring 1998 on the subject "metaphors and models." Gustafson's book *Treasure in*

Earthen Vessels: The Church As Human Community (University of Chicago Press, 1961) was one of the original inspirations for my interest in congregations. I also think of my many visits with Calvin and Nelia Kimbrough on the visual arts and ministry, and with Joseph Gillespie on metaphor and imagination, that have encouraged my thinking about poetics. Students in my regular course "Understanding the Congregation" have brought many questions and reflections that helped shape my ideas.

Finally, I acknowledge my dear friends Ken Gottman and Bob Reber, with whom I've enjoyed many years of lamenting and picking over the state of the church and ministry, after which we have all gone right back to it because we love it and can't let it go. They are both an encouragement to me beyond what I can say here. I look to each of them as exemplary of particular ministries, Ken as pastor, Bob as educator. I dedicate this book to them.

The Soul of the Congregation

June 15

Dear Ken,

I've been getting your sermons and newsletters from Mayflower Congregational every week now for ten years. Both you and the congregation seem to be thriving. The people support a remarkably varied program for a church of a thousand members. Mayflower is known for its ministry of outreach to your community and other places, for grand musical events and dignified worship, and for refreshingly direct and well-researched preaching. The church already has a graceful sanctuary and handsome facilities that will be enhanced now by the capital improvements campaign.

At the same time, your congregation with its complex program and particularly with its name reminds me of the immense pressures on all churches in American society to fulfill a social function essential to the well-being of our communities. The United States is still a relatively new society. Most of the families of this land are within a few generations of being immigrants from somewhere else. Congregations have traditionally been bearers of culture: they have enabled immigrant groups to sustain the practices—food, icons, clothing, language—that continue their familiar culture.

Congregations help people find their place, encourage them to make a place, and comfort them when they do not fit a place. They are sanctuaries of preparation for entering the marketplace of competition. They are zones of solidarity and consolation, giving people solace and language for sustaining individual and family vitality in a social milieu of constant striving.

I saw this social role vividly enacted one Sunday morning of my last pastorate in St. Louis. I got to the church about eight as usual, only to discover the mid-city streets around the building already full of cars. Our programs didn't start till nine-thirty; what was going on? I noticed a flatbed truck parked down the street in front of the neighboring synagogue. It dawned on me that this was the weekend I'd read about in the community paper when Congregation B'nai Amoona was going to move farther out into the suburbs.

In between my last-minute preparations for worship I kept an eye on the street. At about ten, just before our United Methodist service was to begin, the procession got under way. To the sound of a ramshorn and singing, here came the elders of the congregation. They were bearing the ornate Torah scrolls in their arms. They took seats on folding chairs arranged on the truck bed. Finally, with a signaling sound of the horn, the truck began to roll toward the corner and the main street to the western suburbs. Dozens of carloads of synagogue members fell in behind. They were leaving the intersection we had shared for many years.

By that time I had only a moment to grab my robe and rush into the sanctuary to begin our service. I almost couldn't speak for my grieving this exodus. I asked my congregation to pray for God's blessings on the journey of the B'nai Amoona people as they went forth bearing God's Word in their arms. But then I said something like this: meanwhile, we are staying here. Our vocation is to remain in this city at this corner and to be a witness here. We have a place to serve right here in this community. And we ask God's blessing on this place as well.

Much literature on congregations is calculated to help them achieve the social task of moving on, not staying put. In fact, most of it shares the basic market assumptions of the larger culture. Books proliferate on seven-day-a-week programmatic schemes, twelve-step management plans, ten ways to grow in membership numbers. Even literature purporting to address larger cultural issues is oriented to enlightening churches about "new paradigms," new systems enabling more rapid change, or typologies and grids by which to evaluate and improve upon one's own standing.

In short, church management and growth literature—universally calling for new visions and "paradigms" of church—mostly tries to smooth the way for a better fit between congregations and the master narrative of American culture: progress. Change is always good; mobility is always improvement; the future is always an advance over the past.

This narrative—the old, modern framework hardly to be called new or postmodern but only more of the same, for more than two hundred years now—dominates writing and most forms of rhetoric about the churches. It is inseparable from the rhetoric of crisis so predominant in mainstream Protestantism in recent years. Frantic over statistics showing smaller gross numbers of members, these denominations have bought into a rhetoric of bipolar choices—change or die, win or lose, life or death, reform or "the suicide of liberal Christianity," to quote the title of a recent silly book. Reflecting the anxiety of our times, this rhetoric seems to pervade almost every meeting, class, or sermon. And it distracts churches from the more subtle and insidious danger that they will lose touch with their soul—the heritage of traditions and experiences, the wisdom of a collective life lived over generations, and the arts of expressing their faith that make them who they are.

Much as the progress narrative governs congregational life in America, there is much for which it cannot account. The loyalties, commitments, and passions of participants and leaders are only superficially addressed and marshaled by a framework of progress. Thinking of church as a system of productivity does not reach the depths of what the church is for or why people associate with churches. When participants recite a creed or sing a hymn from memory, when they kneel at an altar rail, when they give a Saturday to cook food for the homeless, something else is going on that can only be addressed with a narrative not of progress but of presence, not of productivity but of place.

What bothers me most about many books on the church is that they do not feed my soul. They do not address the memories and hopes, gifts and arts, that constitute my call to ministry. Nor do they touch the collective soul of the congregation. The soul is the meeting place of self and world. It is the ground of expression, of friction among choices and standpoints, the place where I make a life. I express my soul as I make my home, get involved in my neighborhood, do creative and constructive work with hand and word. My soul grows as I seek "the sacred dimension of everyday life," in Thomas Moore's words.

Contemporary Western societies are dominated by the literalism of technology. We are taught to trust only what we know empirically through our senses. We are constantly in search of complete explanations for every phenomenon. We are always measuring one another by race, age, gender, and economic class, fitting people into social pigeonholes. If I want to know you, though, I have to get beyond types and learn your story, the narrative through which you make your life in all its twists and turns, ambiguities and uncertainties.

We are not accustomed to thinking of collective groups like congregations as corporate wholes. As literalists we are taught that groups are only the sum of the individuals who compose them. But congregations as intergenerational communities that stay together over time have their own corporate being, their own unique ways of expressing themselves and living in their world. They spin a rich and complex narrative; they make symbols; they weave a fabric of relationships; they carry out practices of worship, fellowship, and service using the cultural materials available to them.

Congregations can enter this fertile ground of collective soul by exploring their own stories, symbols, rituals, and practices as they have evolved over generations of experience. Immersing themselves in their own culture not only opens new levels of self-understanding of what they are about and why they persist. Deeper self-awareness also reveals new sources of imagination—ways to imagine both the resources of the past (the heritage) and the senses of what a congregation can be for in today's context. Self-knowledge helps a congregation see how it actually does express collectively both the soul of the people gathered and the Holy Spirit's presence in the world.

Church literature based on the paradigm of productivity and technical literalism would have us believe that all congregations are basically alike and therefore are competing with one another on the same statistical racetrack. As you well know, of course, the arts and practices through which your congregation expresses its faith are indeed generically similar to those of other churches, but they are also profoundly different. Indeed every congregation is unique. Certainly the soul does not need every congregation to be the same. The soul thrives on contemplating difference, for if I see your place and symbols clearly, I can see my own more distinctly as well. Then we can talk together more searchingly about what it means to make church today.

Our desire for a deeper understanding of congregational life leads us beyond the literalisms of a production society into the realm of poetics. I mean by poetics not just the study and writing of poems but more broadly the sources of imagination that feed our lives. Poetics is an art of paying attention. Like all the arts, in Moore's words, "It is about arresting life and making it available for contemplation." Poetics requires interrogating basic dimensions of understanding, the framework of time and space through which we ordinarily understand our lives. It requires attending to where we are, including the natural world. This is no mean task in a culture of mobility like ours.

Richard Nelson helped me see this by contrast with the Koyukon culture of the Pacific Northwest. In *The Island Within* he explained that the Koyukon elders

> spent their lifetimes studying every detail of their natural surroundings, and have combined this with knowledge passed down from generations of elders before them. The more people experience the repetitions of events in nature, the more they see in them and the more they know, but the more they realize the limitations of their understanding. I believe this is why [the] Koyukon people are so humble and self-effacing about their knowledge. And I believe that [the] Koyukon people's extraordinary relationship to their natural community has emerged through this careful watching of the *same* events in the *same* place, endlessly repeated over lifetimes and generations and millennia. There may be more to learn by climbing the same mountain a hundred times than by climbing a hundred different mountains.

These are hard words for people jaded by jet travel, glutted with fast food and information, restless, unattached, ready to move on. Poetics requires that we stop and balance our perpetual motion with attention to "the same mountain" of our place. Poetics demands a rigor of plain language, of saying what is really here. It is a discipline of accurate description, of simplicity that is the only way to wipe the lens of incarnation. It is showing, not telling; offering signs, not making. Poetics in congregational life entails a mode of worship, preaching, teaching, and community-making that is first a way of being, not didactic or productive. This makes administration as much presence-being-witness as it is producing-building-recruiting. Poetics offers imaginative resources for fresh understanding of a congregation's culture as well as an enriched vision of congregational presence as a sign and catalyst for God's reign of well-being and justice in the world. Poetics names and expresses, reflects and reinforces the soul of the congregation.

I hope that as you read these letters and reflections you will come away pondering more about who congregations are and what they are for, and with a method for seeing congregations that is imaginative and refreshing. I am convinced that by learning their congregation's culture well, pastors and church leaders can more effectively name the gifts of the people and lead them to build on their strengths for witness and service. This exploring and reflecting is itself an act of ecclesiology, imagining the congregation in a new frame of reference.

Anyway, Ken, please forgive my excesses, feel free to take any insights here and run with them, and join me in the work of the soul for a while. We are, after all, as friends and as congregations composing a life together, a space of presence, freedom, wholeness, and justice. This is what the church has to offer as witness to God's reign.

Tom

Balancing
Perspectives on
Congregational
Life

Reflections

Congregations in the Marketplace

The time has come to explore and understand congregational life in a way that is significantly different from most literature on the "market"—which is just the right term. The books, tapes, Web pages, and seminars that "sell" are the ones that help people "get things done." Although a lot of it is "useful" (I'm using quotation marks as a way of paying attention to the import of the usual choice of words), the predominant methods tend to omit or overlook the dimensions of congregational life that most profoundly shape its character. Church management and marketing literature generally addresses little of the imaginative life that forms the deepest attachments of participants, feeds the theology, witness, and service of a congregation, and helps in understanding what it is like to be part of a particular congregation and what sustains it across generations.

I devote a lot of my time to helping churches "work" better. I teach an introductory course on church administration and leadership for ministerial students. I direct a certification program for people training to be more effective church business administrators as a full-time profession. The need for these courses is growing exponentially. Just in my twenty years as an ordained elder in The United Methodist Church I have seen amazing changes in the scale of church management. Even a medium-sized congregation of, say, four hundred members, is likely to have half a million dollars of income and expenditures in a year. You can't hire a staff anymore without knowing the ins and outs of employment law. The nursery shouldn't have workers, even volunteers, who have not had a background check on their personal histories.

Recent years have brought an amazing proliferation of books and workshops on church finance, personnel management, and building campaigns. Consulting groups and business corporations have sprung up all over the United States and many other countries to provide services to congregations ranging from computer networking to demographic data collection to marketing strategies. Denominations and parachurch organizations offer an enormous variety of workshops directed toward increasing membership and expanding program options. "The church" gives every appearance of being a growth industry.

I'm not surprised about this phenomenon, though it has accelerated faster than I anticipated. Obviously leaders of congregations are looking for resources, and plenty of organizations have sprung up to provide them. Both customers and suppliers of these services have ridden the crest of a strong U.S. economy that has allowed many congregations to expand right alongside other organizations and enterprises in their towns, suburbs, and cities.

What does surprise me is how dominant a utilitarian commercial perspective on church has become. Few authors or church leaders seem to question the thoroughly American assumption that a "real" congregation is most basically an independent economic entity with a building, a bank account, and a paid professional staff, incorporated as a nonprofit organization that is expected to be self-sufficient and self-perpetuating. Traditions of church as an organic unity signified by the Mass and the episcopal office and priesthood (e.g., Roman Catholic, Anglican), or as a connectional system unified by shared ministry and mission (e.g., Methodist, Presbyterian), have a difficult time holding their place in the onrushing stream of congregation-as-independent-economic-unit (most clearly expressed in "free church" traditions).

What matters most in market economies is growth, of course, which means that the churches considered "successful" are growing in numbers, facilities, dollars raised, and variety of programs. A congregation's "mission" to share life in Christ with new people gets all tangled up with organizationally driven goals for expansion. Consequently, for examples of "success," few people look to a congregation of a hundred participants with a thriving ministry in an urban neighborhood, or a church at which a few dozen new immigrants gather to sustain life and hope. What "counts" in the religious, as in the general, economy is innovation that brings big results.

Little wonder that the most publicized examples of vital congregational life are independent congregations, many of which have not even had their second pastor yet, that started with ten persons meeting in someone's home and now have ten thousand or more members gathering in enormous auditoriums or "worship centers." The extraordinary attention paid to these "megachurches" is the master narrative of commercialism writ large in church life. I don't question the authenticity of the faith experience of participants or their generous outpourings of aid to people in need. At the same time, I can't help noticing the parallels between the narrative of McDonald's franchises with their billions of burgers sold and many strategies of church growth. In fact, there are plenty of consultants out there who argue that McDonald's or Microsoft or other styles of innovative enterprise and entrepreneurship are precisely the model for churches of the future.

Many congregations have devised "mission statements" to express their purpose. The most constructive part of this exercise is the actual writing of it, because in order to compose a statement the participants have to focus on what they value most in their congregation's work. I'm not sure such statements mean much to people who didn't participate in actually writing them. To me as an outside reader they seem generic and don't capture much of anything distinctive to a particular congregation.

But having a "mission" is the *sine qua non* of American organizations these days. My local post office, bank, grocery store, hospital, and school all have mission statements posted on the wall or prominently displayed in their literature. Advocates of such statements argue that they help organizations stay focused on their purpose by providing a plumb line for measuring potential actions and avoiding what is not really central. A clear mission statement reminds the organization of its "niche"—what it does well and whom it serves.

Mission statements assume a marketplace in which consumers are making choices based on service or product effectiveness. Thus organizations are competing with one another to offer the "scarce" resource of an excellent product or service well rendered. Just as the consumer looks for a clean grocery store with attractive displays and wide varieties of foods, all at reasonable prices with short lines at check-out, so the consumer looks for a nicely painted and carpeted sanctuary with a cry room for infants, a clean and well-lighted nursery, and a convenient parking place.

As a critical consumer myself, I stay away from dingy grocery stores, and I can certainly understand young parents looking for a nice nursery. What bothers me is the subtext of the marketplace, that if an organization fulfills its mission and competes well it can control its own destiny. The United Methodist Church, for example, has placed in its denominational book of order the statement that "the mission of the church is to make disciples." It then describes a systemic process of inviting people into the church, relating them to God, helping them grow in discipleship, and sending them out into the world in ministry. I hear little discussion, though, of the metaphor of "making." A "disciple" begins to sound like the church's product. And the more of these disciples a church produces, the more it will grow, gain notoriety, and win awards at the regional conference. As ethicist Susan Parsons put it in a recent paper, this mission model "assumes that those with the strongest beliefs and firmest commitment will be furthering God's purposes in the world and will actually be able to bring people to God."

I think it's more than coincidental that the mandate for mission statements has arisen in the years leading up to the year 2000. Millennium frenzy has gripped most business corporations, nonprofit organizations, and denominations since the 1980s. As I write, the year 2000 is practically tomorrow, and the leverage of millennial patter is just about gone. But it has expressed well the ideology of progress with its astonishing hubris that the expansion of a business or a church today will set the time line for a whole millennium.

The books of the past decade that advocate "church marketing" advance two main premises. First, the church is competing with other organizations and activities for people's time and attention. Without more effective marketing, the church will lose "the battle to effectively bring Jesus Christ into the lives of the unsaved population," as George Barna put it. Second, the church must recognize the voluntary exchange relationship that underlies most human activity. If an organization offers a service that meets the needs and desires of its consumers, they will respond in exchange, with participation, money, leadership, or other goods. In order to thrive, then, a church must survey people's needs, evaluate the services it is providing, and seek constant improvement in its service delivery.

A congregation should present "its core doctrines, ministries, and programs [from the] user's perspective," wrote Norman Shawchuck and others, "rather than the seller's perspective, of what constitutes value in the offering." In a "user-friendly" church the "consumer" decides what has value. Traditions such as hymns, creeds, liturgies, and symbols are optional if they do not meet the self-perceived needs of a participant. "Think of your church," continued Barna, "not as a religious meeting place, but as a service agency—an entity that exists to satisfy people's needs." Or to pick up the lingo of other books, congregations must compete effectively to offer "full-service" programming in the "seven-day-a-week church" if they expect to be around for the "new millennium."

In a commercial culture like America's, one can hardly deny that there is a grain of truth in these assumptions. I do begin to worry, though, when a suburban Atlanta megachurch sings Meredith Willson's 1950s song for their benediction each Sunday.

> May the good Lord bless and keep you,
> whether near or far away,
> may you find that long awaited golden day today.
> May your troubles all be small ones
> and your fortune ten times ten.
> May the good Lord bless and keep you
> till we meet again.

What do singers of these words imagine as they sing? Metaphors of gold and fortune are quite literally apropos for the upwardly mobile middle class in suburban Atlanta. Does the church offer any place to stand outside the market—outside the whirl of making and getting and spending? Can the church find any way to talk about a fulfilled life that is not synonymous with progress, growth, rising income, social status, and consumption?

I realize that when congregations are organized in a predominantly commercial culture like America's, they are going to take on some features of the enterprises around them. They have to do some things to get people's attention in a culture surfeited with commercial messages and media. Church leaders have to adapt some skills and learnings from other organizations in order to help congregations function more effectively.

The problem comes when functional utility is taken to be the defining narrative explaining what the church is and why its participants are there. A congregation may have a new sanctuary for worship, but it does not necessarily follow that people gather there for an "exciting worship experience"—they may come seeking the Holy. Even if people do come to a church because they read an advertisement, it does not follow that they are there to meet a specific "need." I don't really understand what most of my "needs" are anyway—that's part of why I continue to listen to Jesus.

Too few leaders in the churches seem to name this dominant commercial framework for what it is, or question its relationship with scripture, traditions, or experiences of church. Shouldn't the discordance jar some critical thought? The price mechanism of the market requires that resources be perceived as scarce (and advertising exists to increase demand); the Scriptures teach that God's love is infinite and abundant. The market supports competition and rewards winners; most churches seek to teach mutual support in community. The market advocates control, planning, and targeted goals of success; the gospel teaches self-sacrifice and service.

In short, commercial utilitarianism is simply not

adequate to understand or explain the church. It reduces the person to an insubstantial shadow of needs and appetites without the dignity of character or heritage. It diminishes the one thing congregations most have to offer in a contemporary-minded culture: the riches of spiritual traditions that have grown up across the centuries. It leaves a congregation as a franchise in a service industry, completely missing the remarkable imaginative life of a community of persons who stay together over time, practicing a faithful way of life together.

Reflections

The "Real" Church

I've just returned from teaching a seminar with about thirty pastors. The announced topic was church polity and organization, and several of them told me that they had almost decided not to come because of it. Who wants to waste two valuable days talking about the constitution and ordered life of churches? I get that reaction to a lot of academic courses I teach, too. Students are always telling me that they dread registering for "church administration."

This initial resistance to learning about church as institution exposes the divided mind of the church. "Up" here we have the "spiritual" and "down" there the "temporal," to use the older rhetoric. Here we have the eternal verities, and there the matters that have fallen into time. Here we have the church at worship and prayer, and there the church raising money and repairing a building. Here we have the pastor inspired to unfold the scriptures from the pulpit. There we have that wretched personnel committee battling again over what exactly the liability insurance policy covers.

The split is constructed into church buildings. Here is the sanctuary replete with rich colors of stained glass or brilliant red carpet, the shiny brass of cross and candlestick, and a cloak of silence. There is the church office corridor, bleached gray-white with flourescent lighting, lined with doors to discrete offices for specialized functions, the air punctuated with sputtering telephones, screeching fax tones, roaring photocopiers, and the plastic staccato of computer keyboards. Are both of these spaces "church"?

The divided mind is embedded in language as well. Before the altar one hears the evocative metaphors of faith practices—"the doors of the church are open," "come to the feast of love," "the fountain of grace flows for you." In the office are the metaphors of the dominant commercial culture, so common one hardly hears them—"he hit the jackpot on that one," "she's not a team player," "who's the audience for this program?" "what's the bottom line in this proposal?"

Various strategies for coping with this double-mindedness have emerged over the years. Pastors have learned to be multilingual, nimble in using each language at the appropriate time. Laity have too often learned that their safest strategy is to leave the "spiritual" metaphors to the "professionals," and to preface any forays into such language with the phrase, "I'm not a theologian, but . . ." Both pastors and laity are liable to fall into a merely utilitarian outlook on their church's institutional needs, keeping them separate from their sense of vocation and spirituality.

Meanwhile the double-mindedness is reinforced by church institutions. People who study, teach, and write "theology" as their profession usually work in seminaries or college and university religion departments.

They necessarily define theology as a field within the academy in conversation with other disciplines, philosophy and the human sciences in particular. With their main attention drawn to the questions most lively among scholars, they tend to view immediate church issues as hopeless tangles, annoying distractions, or problems that could be resolved quickly if people just weren't so narrow-minded. Conversely, the "practitioners" who are trying to lead congregations often do not have or take much time to read theological books or analysis of church and society. They may consider such ideas an "ivory tower" hopelessly out of touch with the press of reality.

The double mind also produces two different literatures about the church. On one side are the "practical" books that show readers how to plant, grow, market, organize, manage, revolutionize, and lead congregations. On another shelf are books—not nearly as many—that address the church from a theological standpoint. Do both of these literatures count as "ecclesiology"? Church-related publishers divide titles as either "professional" or "academic" in nature; is ecclesiology both?

Truly we have gotten ourselves into an awkward fix. The church doesn't seem particularly central to the work of theology and vice versa. Many theologians seem to have abandoned the churches as they actually exist, leaving the field of church literature to the assumptions and dynamics of competitive commercialism. Even our language about church, at least in American Protestantism, is a dry well of functionalism and sentimentality.

If we are going to think constructively about the nature and purpose of the church, we have to find some new standpoint. But to get there we are going to have to clear our heads of the dualistic framework that bedevils us. Not only church management literature but also theology and ecclesiology have reflected this dualism. For most of this century we have been treated to a steady diet of assertions that God acts in the world and uses the churches only insofar as they are in accord with God's mission in the world. Advocates of this view insist that those who serve God outside traditional church institutions are in fact abiding in the fellowship of the New Testament *ekklesia*. The Body of Christ, wrote Swiss theologian Emil Brunner in 1953, "has nothing to do with an organization and has nothing of the character of the institutional about it." Rather it is "a fellowship of persons" brought into being by "their common sharing in Christ and in the Holy Ghost." Historical churches represent a continual falling away from this New Testament *koinonia*, which "was not a 'church' and had no intention of being a 'church.'"

This is the Protestant principle of critique of idolatry in all forms brought to its logical conclusion: no actual church can qualify as the "real church." Luther, and Tyndale before him, would not even use the word "church" (or *Kirche*) in their biblical translations of the New Testament word *ekklesia*. They substituted *Gemeinde* (fellowship) or "congregation" in order to avoid all the overlay of assumptions accruing to the institutional church. These days, of course, many theologians have simply anglicized the Greek to invent the words "ecclesia" and "ecclesial," again inviting the implication that any actually existing churches must be transcended. The true ecclesia is ever an ideal in much theological writing, clearest in the New Testament and evident today only in a few communities of believers usually not connected to institutional churches.

The freedom of such views is exciting, to be sure. Every period of reform in the churches' histories looks back to the New Testament and seeks new ways to act on the original infusion of the Spirit. In the eighteenth century, Protestants sought the ideals of the "primitive church"; in recent years Roman Catholic theologian Leonardo Boff coined the term "ecclesiogenesis" to capture the sense of the church coming into being every time the base communities of Latin America gather.

But it's striking to me how much writing on ecclesiology addresses the church as it "essentially" ought to be and either protests or abandons actual churches. "Disappointed by the homely behavior of the local church and embarrassed by its parochialism," in James Hopewell's words, theologians speak of a church true to gospel ideals that remains outside or beyond actual church life. Like people who declare their desire for "community" but are not willing to sacrifice their individualism for any actual community of real persons, many theologians appear to proclaim the mission of the church while withholding commitment to any one form of it. A critical assumption in this bipolar framework is that "church" is conceivable without "culture," that somewhere or sometime—a place out of places or a time out of times—there is an essential "church" invisible and suspended in eternity that in the end is the only "real" church. Human institutions are poor imitations of the true church, this view holds, supported by the oft-cited Pauline saying that "we have this treasure in clay jars" (2 Cor. 4:7). Real church is a treasure untainted by cultural forms; actual churches provoke a shake of the head and a sigh.

For many laity this assumption leads to the conclusion that there must be another church someplace where "they" know how to do "church" better than "we" do in this impossible little parish. What "we" have here surely could not be "church," not with this leaky roof, squawking choir, and dwindling membership. Or alternatively, "we" will hire an "expert" to come tell "us" how to be "church," because there are professionals who specialize in consulting on "effective" churches.

Of course, there are different minds about what

makes an ideal church, too. To what exactly does "the New Testament *ekklesia*" refer? For some people church is defined by the descriptions of the first Christian community in Acts 2 and 4. Signs and wonders were a daily occurrence, and "all who believed were together and had all things in common; they would sell their possessions and goods and distribute the proceeds to all, as any had need. . . . they . . . ate their food with glad and generous hearts, praising God and having the goodwill of all the people" (2:44-47). For others the ideal church is composed only of those who have walked the Damascus road, knocked from the steed of their past life by the swift and terrible sword of salvation. For others the church is the table of the Last Supper, where the true disciples eat the bread and drink the cup with their Lord. For still others, only the sending of the seventy really counts, as believers go out to preach the gospel to an unbelieving world. Whatever the ideal put forward, "church" is always something more or other than the actual institutions called churches that never measure up.

Certainly one would have to say that actual New Testament churches fit none of these ideals. The ink was hardly dry on the story of communal sharing in Acts 4 when Ananias and Sapphira came into the room one by one, confessed their withholding of some proceeds from a land sale, and fell dead on the spot (the ultimate stewardship sermon). Paul's letters addressed manifold problems in the first Christian communities—misunderstandings among Jews and Gentiles in Galatia, food fights in Corinth. The Revelation to John exhibited all his frustrations with people actually trying to be church in the seven cities (Revelation 2–3).

If we have no ideal church to which to turn, what then shall we do? We will have to quell our perpetual restlessness with present circumstance and be where we are. We are at an odd impasse, with an obsession for making an impact on history driving us one way ("the purpose-driven church") and a fear of getting stuck in history pushing us another ("the cultural captivity of the church"). Questions of history and becoming spur us to seek the ideal church. They lead us to read the Incarnation primarily as God's action in history to which we must respond with activities of our own, with the culmination of history always on the horizon. Questions of heritage and being, by contrast, spur us to ask constantly how God's presence is already incarnate among us in the communities and institutions we have.

The apostle Paul is often cited as exemplary of the church's mission of constant movement to reach new peoples and make disciples under the immediacy of the end of time. But we must be careful not to twist Paul into the frame of our own culture. His peripatetic ministry was balanced with a sense of place as well. This is most evident in his sermon on the Areopagus recorded in Acts 17. Protestant preaching on this passage hammers away with Paul's assertion that God "does not live in shrines made by human hands" (v. 24). But Paul was not only speaking against idols. He was also declaring an incarnational God.

"From one ancestor," Paul went on,

> [God] made all nations to inhabit the whole earth, and [God] allotted the times of their existence and the boundaries of the places where they would live, *so that* they would search for God and perhaps grope for [God] and find [God]—though indeed [God] is not far from each one of us. For "In him we live and move and have our being." (vv. 26-28, emphasis mine)

Our places are a gift from God *so that* we will have a means for seeking God among us. God's presence comes at the places in which our lives meet in community with others and with God.

God doesn't need our sanctuaries. God scallops

the arches of the universe for God's space; God has the stars for a chandelier, the spinning planets for music, the clouds for windows of image and light. We are the ones who need sanctuaries and build them in hope that by gathering week after week in this one place, the God of all creation will grant us a glimpse of grace. Shaped by this landscape of redemption and hope, we go out to live justly in a striving, broken land, our lives centered by trust that the incarnate God will meet us.

"Much as we may wish to be ubiquitous," wrote John Vannorsdall, "everywhere proclaiming the gospel and healing the wounds of the world, most of us will instead be limited, at least for the present, [to the place where] our community is located." So we must attend to where we are—what kind of place this is, what kind of people we are. The dominant culture has instilled in us a deep resistance to such questions, however. As Vannorsdall continued, "The God-appointed seasons of our lives, the boundaries of our habitation[—]To the world, these are the enemies of human life and freedom. But to us, who live by the reversals of God, time and geography are the God-furnished setting within which God comes in search of us." Being church is a real test of faith; it forces us to examine our assumptions and consider a richer, more balanced framework for viewing the world and apprehending God.

Reflections

On Practices

The reluctance of many books on the church to accept actual congregations on their own terms is a rhetorical issue that ought to be taken very seriously. Rhetoric signifies a desired reality from the standpoint of the speaker. In order to write of what they consider to be "vital" or "missional" or "church-of-the-future" congregations or behaviors, authors contrast their ideal model to what actual congregations are like and show how to impose it on these recalcitrant organizations (labeled "old-paradigm" or "dinosaurs"). What congregations do must always be interpreted through a theory from outside of them, and what they "ought" to do must always borrow from other kinds of organizations. In other words, the language native to the congregation is never adequate; some other linguistic world composes the "real" interpretation and program of church.

There are many consequences of this insistence on reframing church in other language forms. For one thing, it regularly leads to the adoption of a model language alien to the congregation but intended to save it. I think of the proliferation of the term "triangulation" from family systems theory, for example, or "quality" from the total quality management method. Such languages constitute a rhetoric of power, not power arising from within the congregation, but power asserted over it by models from outside that redefine the reality of church in words other than the congregation's own.

I would argue that this rhetorical issue is also an epistemological error, a conceptual mistake of fundamental consequence. Many studies appear to impose other languages on their "subjects," describing congregations in terms the congregations themselves would never recognize. This constitutes a claim that a certain theory, then, is more "real" than the congregation's view of itself.

This oft-repeated error was exposed cleanly by the French social scientist Pierre Bourdieu. Models of reality, he said, often slip over the line to become models as reality. The description of behavior becomes the actor's intent, so that when people act they are imputed to be executing the model. Bourdieu called this an "imaginary anthropology." He was especially hard on economists and political scientists who use "rational choice" models based on what a "rational" person would do under certain circumstances. But not only are people not (only) rational; they do not necessarily make choices on the basis of the reasons claimed by a model. Economic models applied to the church (very popular these days) impute motives to the "rational actor," asserting that people actually choose a church because it offers a scarce commodity—a motive that few church members would claim as their own.

We all fall regularly into the "objectivist" error of replacing reality with a model. Family systems theory may bring insight in saying that some persons function as "parents" in organizations, exercising an authority to which other people play "children" as unquestioning followers. But when I use the sentence "He is a parent in this church," the reality claim of the model has begun to replace the model-as-frame for describing what is observed. Or a denominational office might use the term "transitional church" to describe a congregation that was traditionally white in membership worshiping in an increasingly black neighborhood. But when executives speak the sentence, "Mt. Olive is a transitional church," they are now turning reality into the model. Not only might a member or pastor of the congregation argue in response that all congregations are transitional by nature. One might also insist that the implication of this term— people want a church to be either white or black—is profoundly racist and not necessarily descriptive of the actual motives of members, whose practices might lead them toward becoming a multiracial church.

Another way to say this is that models or types of church often get confused with being church. The description or typification of practices begins to substitute for the practice itself. Church growth literature purports to define steps or proven principles of how to grow a congregation. Despite the many examples provided from actual congregations to support models of growth, the models take on a life of their own not connected to any particular congregation. Soon congregations are said to be practicing the model or striving to become a certain type of church—indeed they are urged to do so—instead of simply doing the things that the authors of the models first observed and then typified. Thus the model loses touch with what people are really doing when they "go to church" and with the practices through which people make church together. The church cannot practice numerical growth; it can practice being church as faithfully as possible, and growth may come as a fruit of that practice.

To speak of practices opens up a constructive middle ground between theories coming from outside the congregation on the one hand, and a complete immersion in daily activities and business on the other. Practices give grounds for reflection about actions while staying close to the people and communities who enact them. When I speak of worship, hospitality, music, or prayer as a practice, I am naming a way of doing things that can only be seen in practice among particular communities of faith.

Practices include but are much more than actions. Practices have a history; they are ways and patterns of "doing" that develop over time in continuing communities. Practices sustain and carry forward traditions, bringing together the heritage of a local congregation with the heritage of larger denominational and confessional groups. Practices constitute or bring into being the congregation as it is. Through its practices, a congregation forms a life recognizably distinct from other organizations. It becomes known as a place in which certain practices are carried on, some of which are more widely shared, some unique to that particular congregation. Practices address critical needs of human life and "have practical purposes," as Craig Dykstra and Dorothy Bass suggested. "Oddly, however, they are not treasured only for their outcomes. Just taking a full and earnest part in them is somehow good in itself . . . [participants] are doing it not just because it works (though they hope it does), but because it is good." Practices are more than functional or instrumental means for achieving results. They are a kind of witness, together constituting a distinctive way of life.

Dykstra went further, in another essay, to build on language from the philosopher Alasdair MacIntyre. Practices inherently have their own "histories . . . reasons, insights, values, and forms of judgment." I like the example of baseball. Strategies for choosing to throw a fastball or a change-up, for stealing a base or diving for a line drive, all have their reasons. A player can get better only through practice in these decisions. In fact, as Dykstra and Bass suggested, practices have inherent "standards of excellence" that help us tell a poor practitioner from an excellent one.

Dykstra took this desire for excellence to mean that congregations need to "know what they are doing and why as they engage in [their] practices." He called on pastors to be the primary teachers of these reasons. Here, too, I worry about edging too close to a rationalist error. People generally do not "do" the church's practices because they first know all the reasons for them. Theological and historical analysis of prayer does not necessarily lead people to pray. People learn to pray by practicing forms called "prayer," and they experience prayer itself as a gift, something received.

More broadly, people generally do not adopt a

set of beliefs called "Christianity" and then pick out a church in which to express them. People become "Christian" by practicing a variety of activities enriched by traditions and cultures of the faithful across the generations—worshiping, singing, praying, eating, reading scripture, visiting the sick, helping the needy. But practices cannot simply be deduced from objective conditions. I do not worship because there is a need for worship in the world. I worship because it is a way of life. My life may be a mess of shame and disappointment; but those conditions do not necessarily eventuate in my praying. When I do worship and pray, though, I find myself welcomed into a whole world of practice—language, tune, symbol, story— that I learn more fully only over time. As Bourdieu put it in one of his most delightful sentences, "It is because subjects do not, strictly speaking, know what they are doing that what they do has more meaning than they know."

The rising interest in practices is encouraging because it helps bridge the terrible gap in Western cultures between ideas and institutions, or between ideals of truth and realities of human action. In terms of the church, a focus on practices offers a dynamic way of seeing "church" as always coming into being in continuity with the past, ever generated by the collective and rooted actions of the faithful. Practices can be observed, though there is much more to them than meets the eye. Practices can be reflected upon, though they are resistant to objectification because they are living realities. Practices can help us understand congregations as generative communities that enact or embody Christian faith and defy the common dualism of pure doctrine and cultural captivity.

To put it another way, practice is an incarnational term for means of grace by which God is in the world. Every congregation is constituted by practices of seeking, inviting, hoping for God. Every congregation is a participant in the greater human toil, in Hopewell's words, "to knit a human community out of disparate motives and symbols." Thus the "real church" must be discerned and practiced right here out of the cultural materials at hand.

Reflections

The Practices of Church

I wonder how many pastors get up in the pulpit on a Sunday morning and question what on earth they think they're doing. I used to have that sensation regularly when I was facing the same congregation (more or less) week after week. These days I'm always a guest preacher and I know that when my sermon is over I'm leaving town. But the question still hits me hard sometimes. What am I doing here, trying to address all these people with a message that will inspire them, challenge and comfort them, make them face some things, and help them heal? This impossible gospel that is a way of life—is this to be communicated through my words?

Over here is George, whose relationships with his wife and children have been a tangle of mistakes and attempts at forgiveness. There is Sally, who will rush out after the service to make those real estate sales that help drive up the prices and drive out the lower middle class from our church's neighborhood. Scattered here and there are middle managers for one of America's leading defense contractors. Down front as always are John and Dot, retired owners of the corner drugstore that anchored this neighborhood for two generations. Several teenagers have taken up residence in their usual far pew, passing notes, giggling, and staring skeptically as I begin.

We have just sung the Charles Wesley hymn I selected as preparation for the sermon; it was written more than 250 years ago in language that's a bit archaic but speaks truth.

> Help us to help each other, Lord,
> each other's cross to bear;
> let all their friendly aid afford,
> and feel each other's care.
>
> Touched by the lodestone of thy love,
> let all our hearts agree,
> and ever toward each other move,
> and ever move toward thee.

I have this impulse to call a halt after each verse and shout, "Are you listening to these words? Do you know what this means?" Startling them to attention, I would explain how "moving toward one another and moving toward God are a movement in the same direction because the church is a circle centered on God so that as we move closer to one another we are also moving closer to the center, which is an idea the Wesley brothers learned from fourth-century Christians, which means the hymn ties us to the whole Christian tradition and do you people realize that we aren't the first Christians in history to sing and that our voices are joined with the whole communion of saints and isn't that fantastic!" Then I would gasp for air as the entire congregation stood with jaws agape, wondering if they should call the little men in the white coats to come fetch their preacher.

Fantasies aside, the hymn concluded without commentary, I step up, deal out my notecards on the lectern like a riverboat gambler, in Frederick Buechner's image, and open my mouth to speak. It helps to remember that I am certainly not the first and will not be the last to preach the gospel and be terrified.

In all the actions I have just described and more, congregations continue the practices that together constitute the church. I have written that practices are more than just activities, they are part of a way of life that has a history and forms an outlook. When my congregation sings, they continue a practice of singing the faith that has been expressed in every generation of Christianity. People come to worship knowing that they will sing together, for most of them the only time in daily life when they will use their voices in this way. In singing they will experience that unique solidarity of joining voices in a common song, through poetry and melody expressing far more than is possible in ordinary speech. When I preach, I continue a practice that spans centuries of proclaiming the gospel.

Practices are general enough to have names and qualities, but they cannot be separated from their expressions in definite cultural forms. I can recognize preaching but may not understand the language of the preacher. I have experienced hospitality in many different congregations; I know it is hospitality, but here it may take the form of coffee and cakes at a neatly arranged table, there a plate of barbecue beef at a picnic in the churchyard.

Practices are formed in community; even those exercised individually have a communal history in the *ekklēsia*, the New Testament's word for Christian gatherings. *Ekklēsia* is the same term that was used for the town meeting of free, property-owning male citizens in ancient Greece. No one knows exactly how the Christians came to adopt it, but several features commended the term. First of all, it was an assembly, a gathering or coming together for a common purpose. Second, it had implicit in its word root a sense of call *(kaleo)*, that people were called away from other activities to come together for this purpose. Third, the assembly had in view the common good of the whole community.

Christians expanded the ecclesia, of course, to be a gathering of all the people called — male and female, rich and poor, slave and free, Gentile and Jew. They had a new name for the common good, the well-being and justice of all peoples, the reign of God. They were creating a new public open to all who came to hear the gospel and hoped to lead a new life.

Ekklēsia described most immediately the assembly or congregation in each place. Yet the more Paul used the term in his letters, the more he showed that *ekklēsia* was both local and universal at the same time. Paul used the word to describe gatherings in peoples' homes, congregations in cities, all the congregations of a region, and even the whole Christian movement. This conveyed a deep truth that every congregation is fully the church in a place even as each assembly is one expression of a more universally practiced faith. As Hans Küng put it, "The local ekklesia is not a 'section' or 'province' of the whole ekklesia. It is in no way to be seen as a 'subdivision' of the real 'Church.'" Christ is wholly present in each place; the whole gospel is fully available. "The local Church is the Church," Küng continued. "The whole Church can only be understood in terms of the local Church and its concrete actions."

Christian practices that constitute ecclesia are manifold, and each deserves full description and understanding. That would require more than I can write or you can read right now. But I have found it helpful to think about the church's practices through the dynamic of breathing in and breathing out. One moment of breathing in finds the congregation gathered in worship, *leitourgia*, the work *(ergon)* or service of the people *(laos)* of God in a particular place. Worship is work. It is a service the people perform together, into which they must pour their attention and energy for the acts of praise, repentance, proclamation, and offering of themselves.

At the companion moment of breathing out, the congregation is living out another kind of service, now their *diakonia*, their ministry in the world. For this service the Holy Spirit bestows gifts and graces such as teaching or healing, though Paul's lists of spiritual gifts in his letters to the churches are hardly exhaustive. As is well known, one of the most important tasks of ordained ministry is to help order these ministries, that is, "to equip the saints for the work of ministry" (Eph. 4:12). The Greek word for "equip" is *katartismon*, which refers to assembling a puzzle. You have to figure out how to put the right persons in the right places, where they can fully exercise their gifts, and nothing is worse than having the wrongly gifted person trying to fulfill a badly needed ministry. I like Peter's image of living stones, too (1 Pet. 2:5). The building up of the household of faith means fitting together all the differently shaped and sized stones to make a wall aligned on the cornerstone who is Jesus Christ. And some stones are really, really different, you can't help thinking as you look out over your congregation's faces.

A second moment of breathing in begins with the fellowship or community of the faithful in a place. Through mutual care, hospitality, and education the people build one another up in love, again in Ephesians' terms, "grow[ing] up in every way into him who is the head, into Christ" (4:15). There is no greater challenge for congregations than becoming a community. Here I encounter other people who hear things differently, violate my norms, challenge my assumptions, and stretch my understanding. Congregations are a laboratory in public conversation among persons whose competing orbits of meaning cannot be collapsed into a lowest common denominator, yet who can become a community by living and serving together over time.

In the companion moment of breathing out, Christians express the dispositions toward community that have been instilled through the trials of life together in their congregations. Through acts of care and hospitality they seek the same wholeness in their neighborhoods and cities that they have sought in their assemblies. Their practices of community connect them with congregations in many places.

If this discourse on practices is starting to sound like the same idealism about the "real church" that I was protesting before, let me emphasize again that while I can name distinct practices of church, I cannot see them anywhere except as they are expressed in particular cultural forms of actual congregations. There is no church apart from local congregations gathering in certain places. This means that when we say "church" we should not imagine a static structure frozen in eternity, a timeless ideal to which actual congregations only feebly aspire. Nor should we simply call to mind all the embarrassing and exasperating features of congregations we know, and give up on church altogether.

Thinking of church as constituted by practices offers us an alternative to dualism. We can say that church is living and dynamic, that it is always coming into being freshly even as it continues a way of life expressed in many times and places. We can say that if there is no ideal church someplace else, then what we do in the congregations in which we actually participate is of utmost importance. Everything is at stake in the life of the congregation. If we cannot practice the gospel here, then where can we expect to see it? True, God always exceeds our expectations and may show up any number of places in our world. But we are still called to be fully church, fully the people of God, where we are.

I have expressed my concerns about the commercial utility that so dominates our lives in Western societies and our churches. If there is no pure practice, no ideal ecclesia by which to judge today's churches, then from what standpoint can I be critical of congregational practices? In giving up the Christ and culture dialectic, haven't I just forfeited the right to name what I might want to call distortions of the Christian way? This is a crucial issue, because if I can't call evil or sinfulness by name, then I have no alternative but to accept whatever I have in front of me that calls itself church. And to know what evil is, I have to have some standard that transcends times and situations, right?

Otherwise by what norm can I differentiate "good" church from "bad" church? Isn't there such a thing as better worship and worse worship, good preaching and bad preaching? In Dykstra and Bass's terms, isn't there a "standard of excellence" in Christian practices to which all congregations ought to strive? I am appalled by what some congregations do while invoking the name of Jesus Christ. But on what basis can I criticize?

These questions do not spur me to leap to a foundationalist view of truth. Even if we assert some absolute foundational truths about the gospel and the church, we still have to discern those truths in the actual practices that we can observe and in which we participate. If we did get all the assertions of doctrine and all the attributes of a truly Christian congregation written down, then what? Churches have doctrines and creeds, to be sure, but they are distillations of the faith and practice of living communities in continuous formation across generations. Faith has to be lived, and in being lived it becomes increasingly complex and nuanced.

When we ask what exactly is the Christian way, we must turn and face one another. We have to share our struggles to be faithful, talk through our doubts, risk examining what we consider our successes, and experience practices both within our own congregation and others. Self-consciously expressing our own imagination about the church, we can enter empathetically into the imaginative world of others. We can better understand the springs of their imaginative life, even as we give testimony to our own forms of expression. The competitive model of the marketplace drives us away from such conversation, reducing faith to individual choice and pushing congregations toward autonomy. If the ecclesia, though, is an assembly for the common good seeking to practice the Christian way authentically, then it must be a community of Christian conversation.

The practices of Christian congregations are patterns for hearing the gospel again and learning how to live it. Together they form a habit of being and a way of life. They stir and guide the imaginative life that enables participants to empathize with the needs and hopes of others. George, Sally, John and Dot, all the middle managers, and the teenagers are joining at some level in these practices. Their outlooks and dispositions are shaped in varied ways by what they do together in the congregation, even as Charles Wesley and other witnesses from other times and places resonate with their voices. So I guess I'll try the pulpit one more time. Together we can pray to see a little bit more what this Christian faith is about.

An Ethnographic Disposition

June 29

Dear Ken,

This morning I got to thinking about my visit to Grand Rapids last summer. Remember how we decided to ride out to the airport together in my rental car because we both had flights to Atlanta at about the same time, but on different airlines? My plane was going to stop in Detroit on its way south; yours flew to Milwaukee first. We sat in the airport contemplating the roiling gray-black sky in the west and the ugly storms depicted on weather channel radar. As I recall, you later described your flight as something like a ride in a blender. Mine cut along the eastern edge of the front and largely escaped the bumps.

A lot of people don't like to fly because of this serendipity, but let's face it—jet travel is one of the technologies that has absolutely transformed human life. For one thing, when I fly I experience the world as vastly compressed. I walk on board, wearing soft, loose-fitting clothes and gripping my carry-on bag. I lift the bag overhead to a bin, lower my body into an aisle seat (always an aisle), and begin to read. I hear the roar of engines; I catch a glimpse through a nearby window of land falling away; I hear the engines cut back, feel the pressure in my ears, and ride out the bump of the landing. I then walk out of this noisy steel shell and find myself in an entirely different landscape. Little time—only a fraction of a day—has elapsed. I am in the same clothes, carrying the same bag, but everything around me—the land, the sky, the air, the built landscape—is different. I have little sense of having traversed the earth, only of being deposited in a different place.

I've always wondered what it's like for a housefly who comes on board a plane. Enjoying with the rest of us the life-saving benefit of the air pressure system, the fly has a great time dining off the airline food (probably enjoying it more than anyone else) and alighting on people's heads. Later the door opens and the fly exits to find itself—where? What happened to the kids? My favorite garbage can? Where am I? But maybe this is projection.

The other thing about airplanes is that for the first time in human history a great number of human beings have had an aerial view of the world. Every summer of my boyhood, our family would make the trek across the hot plains of Kansas to spend a month at a cabin in the Rocky Mountains. A bag of cold water tied to the front grill of the Nash, we would cruise along with one eye on the temperature needle hoping and praying that it wouldn't get to the red zone again. With the other eye we would play a game of guessing how far it was to the grain silo on the horizon, almost always underestimating by several miles the distance through the mirages of heat. Then came the most important car game with the thrill of being the first to spot the Rockies, harder than one would think with all the clouds that looked kind of like mountains. There was no mistaking them, though, once we were close. They pushed up out of the plain with an urgency and grandeur that made it seem as though they were still growing. Their immensity was fearsome; it still takes me several days to get used to their massive presence when I visit.

At that time, only a tiny percentage of human beings had ever seen the Rockies from above. Nobody I knew had ever looked down on them. Everybody always looked up. But now the mountain sky is criss-crossed all day long with contrails, and many people have flown over the mountains with hardly a glance out the window.

In fact the Rockies are only a small feature in the grand map of America as many people experience it. When I fly from Atlanta to Seattle, in only four hours I traverse nearly the entire breadth of the North American continent. The red clay and pine forests of the Southeast give way to the black soil of river valleys; the high plains with the circles and squares of cultivation suddenly erupt into rugged, snowy peaks; the gashes and rifts of mountain canyons play out into desert, followed at last by a startling row of volcanoes stretching to the northern and southern horizons; and the plane descends to the watery green shores of Puget Sound. It's hard not to burst into a chorus of "This Is My Country." The exhilaration of seeing it all as one molded landscape makes me want to grab a pen and write all about my grand vision from on high.

A lot of books are written in airplanes. At least they give the impression of an aerial view. From the air one has a sense of grasping the big picture. One can decide that there are basically five types of land or essentially seven regions, and one can write general descriptions of those types. One then can wax eloquent about the patterns and trends one sees, even speculating what the future holds unless prescribed changes are made.

A lot of authors in church development literature seem to prefer being pilots. They do, to some extent, poke around on the ground, get stuck in the mud of particularity, and wade through congregational messes. But their real excitement and payoff comes in soaring around with an aerial view, summarizing, generalizing, and forecasting. This is how writing about the church gains credibility; it is more authoritative to survey a thousand churches than to examine one in depth.

From 35,000 feet I can barely see the Appalachian hilltops slashed away by strip-mining, the nuclear power plants punctuating the Ohio River shoreline, the subdivisions of twenty-acre "ranch" lots platted on the Wyoming plain, or the clear-cuts of forests in the Cascades. Certainly I do not see anything of the river-bottom shanties on stilts, or the segregation by class and race in city streets, or the neighbors who will not speak to each other across the lot line.

From the air, the sharp edges of difference get fuzzy and the dense detail of local situations flattens out. Actual people in all their disarray are not visible at all, except as miniatures who, in the scale and proportions of a doll house, illustrate the fashions, plans, and hopes of the theoretical giants who arrange the rooms. In some ways it's a relief to be in the air, to get away from the daily press of these people and their needs. "I can get some distance and perspective," we commonly say, "new ideas and insights." But then the moment of detachment must give way to new engagement.

I have learned a lot from flying, to be sure When I fly to Grand Rapids in the evening, I'm fascinated by the grid of lights strung down the roads in Ohio. It's like a giant electronic display of the Northwest Ordinance land survey from the 1790s. The tracts and sections remain largely unchanged from those early days. The question is, How do I use that knowledge to understand more deeply the situation of a church located at one of those county line crossroads? What does the settlement of this land teach me about the people of this congregation? That's certainly something worth exploring.

Thus what I can learn from the aerial, general izing view is significant only in relation to the particular, ground-level view. Without the reality check of actual congregations and the real people who inhabit them, I am tempted to settle for glib generalizations. Probably no society is more obsessed with demographic data than ours. Gender, ethnicity, age, education, income level, sexual orientation, and place of residence all are markers by which we continually take stock of ourselves. But without attention to the human beings right in front of me with whom I am in relationship, this constant census-taking is oppressive. It reduces people, and their associations such as congregations, to labels and types.

I have found the art of ethnography to be a compelling alternative, a way of paying attention and staying connected to the people and places where I am. Ethnography is simply the study of *ethnā,* people. It is the name for organized, detailed observation of people in all their interactions, gestures, practices, languages, and other cultural artifacts. Ethnography starts with "being there" (the title of a recent ethnographic study of seminaries), watching, noting signals and patterns, entering into the world of a particular group of people as both observer and participant. It is neither possible nor desirable to observe without being observed, to watch without becoming also a participant in the group's activities. Ethnographic research recognizes that the person doing the observing is also altering the reality being studied; but of course that has been shown to be true of much of the physical and social sciences.

Ethnographers are more akin to naturalists than to anatomists. The latter takes a bird to the laboratory, kills it, dissects it, classifies its parts, and studies how they work together to enable the bird to feed, fly, make baby birds, and so on. The naturalist sets up a tent and stool, adjusts the binoculars, and waits—waits and waits—to observe the bird in its habitat. Both approaches contribute to knowledge of the bird, though one must say that when the anatomist is done, the bird is no more and can't be re-created. At least the naturalist can leave after observing, with the bird and its habitat being much the same as they were. Neither approach, blessedly, can answer the question of whether birds sing when they don't have to, or why they are here at all. It does seem to me, though, that the naturalist approach—watching, listening, and wondering—has a better chance of appreciating these mysteries.

Ethnographic studies have provided intriguing, innovative insights into congregations in recent years. The published reports are the product of some very patient people. Samuel Heilman lived and worshiped with an Orthodox Jewish synagogue in suburban Philadelphia for a year; Melvin Williams spent three years with a black Pentecostal church in Pittsburgh; my colleagues Charles Foster and Ted Brelsford and their research team worked with three multicultural congregations in Atlanta intensively for more than a year. What did they do all that time? They went to worship services, sat through religious education classes and sometimes taught them, attended endless board meetings, walked the parking lots to watch people arrive and leave, strolled neighborhood sidewalks, and interviewed dozens of people.

Paying attention is a lot of work. Heilman estimated that every fifteen minutes of observation eventuated in an hour of writing out notes. After observing just one hour-long worship service, I can usually typewrite at least a ten-page single-spaced document simply recording everything I saw and heard. Even then, another member of my observation team will note many words and events that I missed. It's like going to a movie—sometimes we all come out with such different impressions we can't believe we were in the same theater.

Moreover, every encounter is a new window into the congregation's reality. Here's a woman asking me wryly, "Are you observing today, or are you worshiping with us?" Or a man murmuring in my ear from the pew behind after the sermon, "Now you know why we need a new pastor." Or my sudden realization that I'm the only white person in an African American worship service and "everybody's watching me." I can hardly write fast enough to get all these things down, even if I do it afterward (which is preferable).

Sociologist Nancy Ammerman wrapped up her study of a fundamentalist church with hundreds of pages of typewritten notes. She had conducted seventy-eight interviews and a demographic survey to supplement her observations. She devised a topical filing system that enabled her to record her discoveries in an organized fashion and to find items when she wanted them. Heilman ended up with "six volumes of notes," which he eventually thematized only after careful reading and rereading. Others (like me) spread stuff out over big tables and keep circling to recall what's what and how it fits together.

I realize that being a naturalist is not easy when you are the pastor leading the meeting or the layperson teaching the class. But for me, it is one way to break out of my taken-for-granted world and discipline myself to pay attention to what's there. I require students in my congregational studies classes to observe several different events in their respective congregations, even if they are in leadership roles there. Their writing task is to describe whatever they observed in such a way that I as a stranger who has (usually) never been there can "see" it and experience it with them. They find it a tough assignment, but one that almost always rewards them with insights beyond anything they imagined.

Why is it so hard to pay attention? I attribute it

in part to a dominant culture that encourages distraction. Our senses are irradiated with light and noise. We travel across the land at high speeds. We stand in grocery store aisles paralyzed by having to choose among fourteen different kinds of orange juice. We can't bear to wait for anything—every minute must be productive or in motion. How can we possibly concentrate, without deliberate discipline?

We rely on assumptions about our daily life patterns so that we can reduce our sensory intake. If I really noticed whether the morning paper lands on the same crack of my driveway every day, or which clerk waits on me at the fast-food drive-through, or what that faint squeak is that I hear through my office wall, I fear I might go out of my mind. I have enough to think about already.

The first twenty times I entered the church at the beginning of my last pastorate, I couldn't stop looking at the dark stain in the hall carpet that urgently needed replacement, and fussing over the way I had to pull the office door toward me to get the key to turn the bolt. After that, I didn't notice anymore. I began to take my environment for granted.

Moreover, when I arrived as pastor I brought a world of assumptions that I expected and hoped to have confirmed. I assumed that the congregation would have a treasurer and various bank accounts, that a pipe organ would be found in the sanctuary, that there would be a list of "shut-ins" (a metaphor common in many congregations, and a particularly revealing one in a society that idolizes mobility). In short, I came looking for familiar ground as much as for new territory that would demand attention. I brought my churchly images and metaphors with me and looked for ways in which the congregation confirmed them.

Then instead of disciplining my attention, I let

it be guided by the demands of what was new to me. Another way to say it is that what was new to me in the congregation in which I had newly arrived constituted a crisis for me—a crisis of knowledge and skill—and I immediately put my energies into absorbing or normalizing the crisis. But this meant that I was putting little energy or focus on the whole reality of the congregation to which I needed to pay attention.

Later I'll describe some of the actual methods my students and I have found useful in exploring congregations. For now I just want to plead for the fruitfulness of an ethnographic outlook in enhancing ministry. To cultivate the arts of paying attention means to watch deliberately, make notes, conduct interviews structured around questions planned in advance, in short, to push through the facile gloss that comes so readily to us ("this congregation is just like . . .").

An ethnographic disposition helps a pastor hear through the whine ("Pastor Smith always visited people in their homes"), to the need ("I really need a pastor right now"). It opens a way through nostalgia ("I remember when we had sixty kids in youth choir"), to the strengths that endure over time ("This church has always loved music—what are some new ways we could offer the music of faith to our community?").

Most of all, a disposition toward ethnography honors this particular congregation, the one right in front of me, the one I am serving. It says clearly that while this congregation bears some similarities to others I've known, nonetheless it is a unique human community with its own unique story, mix of people, and outlook. Because it is unique, it deserves my full attention, so that I can learn from its particularity how to lead it into the next phase of its life. This congregation was here long before I came (usually) and will be here long after I'm gone. I will honor these people as a collective whole from whom I can learn—and nothing would make them more inclined to honor me than my paying full attention to them.

Some pastors have told me that they don't have time for this approach—there are sermons to preach, programs to install, missions to accomplish. "These people need a fire built under them." Others say that they don't anticipate serving a particular congregation long enough to make this sort of depth knowledge desirable or useful. "Why should I bother learning this much about these folks when I know I'll be leaving in the next year or two?" (These are usually Methodists.) To these perspectives I can only say that paying attention is also a spiritual discipline that not only centers one's life but opens the way to entirely unanticipated dimensions of experience.

Tom

Reflections

Poetics and Imagination

A few years ago I began working on a book about congregations for the Council of Bishops of The United Methodist Church. At the time I first met with the episcopal committee charged with producing a pastoral "foundation document," they had already chosen a title, "Vital Congregations—Faithful Disciples." The title stuck; but nobody knew for sure what the book should say. Most of the bishops were assuming that they should do what denominational leaders generally do, which is to create a program for congregations to carry out. On this view I should write out the ten steps to vitality and eight ways to faithfulness, develop a study guide for each, design a report form for every congregation to turn in to district headquarters, and urge the purchase of larger file cabinets to hold all the paper. In other words, congregations would remain in the passive position, receiving what outside authorities tell them they should do and then quietly (but aggressively) ignoring the program.

Other bishops were determined not to do business as usual. We began to realize that we needed to base the book on the common experience of congregations and to hear their voices. We designed a process called "a gathering for celebration and discovery" through which a congregation could put, in its own words, its understanding of its corporate ministry and mission. We asked members of more than three hundred congregations to tell us what it was like to be a member in their particular congregation and what they viewed the challenges of their congregation and community to be. This produced an outpouring of stories, images, memories, and metaphors, many of which found their way into the document itself. Meanwhile, the bishops adopted a text organized around congregations' most common experience, the sequence of moods and moments in worship—praise, confession, hearing, responding, and so on. The two sources were printed side by side, the bishops' text on congregational vitality closest to the binding of each page, the congregations' voices appearing as a chorus of midrash illuminating the text alongside it.

The congregations' words were astonishing in freshness and insight. Trinity Church in Providence, Rhode Island, wrote:

> If one enters our large sanctuary before the people arrive, there is the distinct feeling that many souls from the past still reside there. The round stained-glass window high above the altar; the mahogany

baptismal urn; the heavy glass and iron chandeliers; the red seat cushions—much was given in memory of church members or their loved ones. The Library in the corner of the sanctuary holds shelves of books dated clear back to the 1800s. There is a picture of the Trinity Union Sunday School in its heyday. The people look like they are related.

We don't know most of these people. They are dead or gone away. Trinity is a new church now. On any Sunday, there are Africans, Afro-Americans, Cambodians, and Anglo-Saxons. On the bulletin board in Fellowship Hall is a photo of each person who registered for our Sunday School last year, black, brown, and white. Above the Sunday School altar is a hand-crocheted picture of Jesus with outstretched hands, a gift from Sr. M. in Liberia. Below the picture reads, "He's Got the Whole World in His Hands."

Church leaders, whether in congregations or denominations, are so accustomed to using powerful languages from outside actual congregations that they may not be confident that there is a "native tongue" worth hearing. Certainly congregations are not accustomed to being asked to speak in their own voice. Yet their language is rich with experience and incarnation. From them, the book claimed, will come "a new imagination for tomorrow's church."

An appeal to imagination brings me to consider the possibilities of a poetics of congregational life. Poetics is a term that refers to poetry, to be sure, in particular the critical analysis of how poetic language works. I wish to include that basic sense of the term, acknowledging the many poetic forms through which Christians have expressed their faith. But I do not here limit poetics to poetry itself.

By poetics I mean the images, metaphors, memories, and reveries that fund the imaginative life of individuals and communities of faith. And because such images usually arise from congregational practices expressed in story, symbol, ritual, and place, I use "poetics" not only to refer to language itself but to encompass the whole range of resources through which the imaginative life may flourish. The church's task of poetics is the critical and constructive use of these imaginative resources in edifying—to use Ephesians' term—or building up and bringing to strength and fullness the whole body of the community of faith.

Poetics is stirring a great deal of interest these days. This is apparent not just in the proliferation of poetry readings in bookstores and displays of poems in public buses and subways. Poetics is a prominent feature of contemporary philosophy, theology, and cultural studies. In one respect it honors a hunger for good language in a culture surfeited with amplified words, commercial jingles, and media sound bites. Poetry readings and church are two of the places one can go these days to be reasonably hopeful of finding language worth hearing.

In a broader, deeper respect the growing love of poetics is a sign of desire for reality—a richer, more multidimensional description and experience of reality than technical and scientific knowledges have been able to deliver. It is not that technological advance has not done much to enhance people's lives, or that the physical and social sciences have not done much to increase understanding of human being and behavior. It is simply that these learnings do not, and cannot, go farther than they do. They cannot feed the soul or the soul's yearnings.

Poetry does not, like the sciences, try to solve problems or delineate the steps to predictable outcomes. Poetics arises out of the ambiguities of life, the irreconcilable opposites that live side by side, the collision and fusion of the real and the unreal to create new knowledge. For recent generations of the dominant American culture—especially in the knowledge class that makes its living by manipulating words and numbers—poetics has been the least recognized of the practices of language. What really counted was what could be empirically demonstrated or scientifically replicated. But now many people are realizing that such knowledge can account for only a small part of life. Most distinctions will not hold; most typologies do not comprehend. "Everything comes alive when contradictions accumulate," wrote the French philosopher Gaston Bachelard. This is the richness and fascination of living.

The point is not to set up an opposition between the scientific and the poetic, or to insist that one must choose between representational or referential language on the one side and poetic language on the other. We need both for a fuller understanding of the realities in which we find ourselves.

Let me try an example that may seem trivial to anyone who has never been a pastor arriving at the church on a January Sunday morning, brilliant sermon tucked in her fist, only to find the sanctuary ice-cold. As pastor of a church with a seventy-five-year-old building, although I learned more about heating and cooling systems than I ever dreamed of knowing, I made it clear that I was not the one to whom to turn in such circumstances. When the church furnace needs repair, the congregation needs to call upon a trained technician who can read the terminology of a manual and handle a plumber's wrench or screwdriver in all the right places. But it remains true nonetheless that when church members refer to the boiler room as "the catacombs" they speak of something equally real, that in the underground guts of a church building reside many ghosts from the past embodied in pieces of crown molding from the last remodeling job, broken chairs from the old youth room, and even (in more than one church I've heard of) the actual crypt of a former pastor or member. When the furnace breaks down, someone has to descend to this underworld and negotiate detente with these spirits.

Poetics calls upon a distinct use of language, to be sure. When we sing, "The church's one foundation is Jesus Christ her Lord," we don't mean that Jesus is downstairs struggling to hold up the whole building on his shoulders—though this is the mental image I always had as a child every time we sang the hymn. Nor do we expect actual flames when the preacher prays for the Lord to send down "the fire of your Holy Spirit"— despite the vividness of the tongues of flame at Pentecost (Acts 2). Poetic speech is less direct than the literal since it calls upon the hearer to suspend "the ordinary reference attached to descriptive language," in the words of philosopher Paul Ricoeur.

Yet we would not be content to say that images of faith are less true than, say, the radiator tag that tells me to turn the knob to the left for more heat and right for less (which always seems backward to me). As Ricoeur put it, "Poetic language is no less *about* reality than any other use of language." In fact, it may be that poetics "constitutes the primordial reference to the extent that it suggests, reveals, unconceals . . . the deep structures of reality to which we are related as mortals who are born into this world and who *dwell* in it for a while." Poetic language has its own precision, of a different sort from literalism, evoking what no other form of language can express.

Poetics invites us into the realm of imagination. This latter term belongs among the many—myth, dream, story would be others—that have been relegated by an empiricist culture to the sphere of the untrue and dangerously unbounded. The main things that "count" are phenomena and actions that can be observed, measured, tallied, and predicted. Other "stuff" that goes on "in people's heads"—the things they imagine—are fleeting fantasies, it is said. Bachelard was even feistier about a claim firmly contrary to this modern assumption. Images, he argued, are "sudden events in life. When the image is new, the world is new." When people imagine reality differently, their world is truly different. An image never before imagined is an actual event, a change of the real. Again, the point is not to set up a polarity or reinforce the divided mind. Our best notions are those "in which the reason and the imagination have been acting in concert," in poet Wallace Stevens's words. Just as a reasoned thought may lead to discovery of a new understanding, so "a poetic idea . . . gives the imagination sudden life." We need each to thrive.

Poetics has a certain affinity with the ethnographic disposition for which I was appealing earlier. Both begin with acute and sensitive observation and require paying constant attention. Both also contain a distancing moment of appraisal and consideration. Poetics flourishes, though, when it moves, perhaps beyond typical ethnographic practice, into an immersion and identification with whatever the "poet" observes, risking full engagement with the imaginative possibilities of the situation. That risk and promise take reflection on the church in a fresh direction.

Communities of faith have a particular stewardship of the poetic. When "church" is reduced to action only and measured by its productivity alone, it becomes beholden to the "principalities and powers" of ideologies. In the context of the dominant American ideology, "church" must always remake itself to contribute to "progress." But I am not proposing a counter-ideology, in which "church" is synonymous with resistance and revolution. I am urging that "church" be considered in its full giftedness, as a community of imagination that through its language signals a new creation.

"The church has a particular obligation to use incarnational language," wrote poet Kathleen Norris. In contrast to languages of "exactitude" and "appraisal," "incarnational language pulls things together." This dynamic is exemplified in metaphor, which, "like the incarnation itself, is a uniting of disparate elements." Driven apart by distinctions of ideology, people of faith need "language rich in ambiguity."

> Poetry, above all, makes room. In our ideological age, making room, especially for those who disagree with us, is a dangerous thing to do. Poetry does not lend itself to ideology [nor is it] designed to convince the reader of a certain point of view. . . . By drawing on metaphor, which yokes together that which the linear intelligence comprehends as disparate, the poetic intelligence might offer us a way to comprehend our essential unity.

The punch line here is not a proposal to create a new professional class of church poets. Nor is it to suggest that only people of poetic imagination belong in church or ministry. The question is how poetics can help congregations gain fresh insight into their corporate lives and imaginative inspiration for their common tasks.

A deep river of images feeds the roots of congregations; the collective imagination expresses itself in a profusion of symbols, stories, rituals, and activities. Thus congregations themselves are springs of theological imagination. They offer the images that extend Christian understandings of God and God's reign in the world. Some images are unique to a particular place and group; some are more widely recognizable. Each congregation expresses its faith in its own characteristic ways, even while drawing on many common elements. In their practices of liturgy, service, and community, congregations both incorporate and extend the living traditions that they bear.

Inherited forms are a rich source of imagination for the church. Today's congregants might not install

Tiffany stained-glass windows depicting scenes in Jesus' ministry or put a sixteenth-century alabaster madonna figure at the center of a worship space. They might not make decisions using Roberts' Rules of Order or put so much time into recruiting volunteers to keep a church parlor clean. Yet it is still possible to honor practices and symbols created from the imaginative life of past generations—their efforts to be church in their own time—in fact to learn from those expressions, to be deepened in one's own imaginings, and then to add one's own contribution.

Exploring inherited images can be painful; many people are alienated from churches because of symbols and actions generated in the past. Here is a congregation with a front hall display of framed photographs of lay leaders and pastors over the years; all have been men, a fact with which women come face to face every time they enter the door. There is a congregation with an eight-foot iron fence topped with razor wire around its property, a symbol of mistrust between community and church. Here is a congregation worshiping in a windowless room of an office building, having sold their old Gothic structure to the state for a highway right-of-way. In all these cases pain may run deep and conflicts endure. The absence of once-active participants, like an amputation, may still throb.

This is the cost of human community that, by trying to practice Christian faith, inevitably creates brokenness and pain. In Hopewell's words, "Although the congregation knits itself together by inspired strands . . . each by the activity of the same congregation also corrupts its nature and threatens the congregation's own life together." Congregations create and lose, make and break. Theology as poetics trusts the hope that even from the brokenness of the past a new imagination can arise for the congregation's life. By bringing their imaginative life to critical awareness and constructive generativity, congregations can engage more faithfully in being and becoming church.

Exploring
Congregational
Culture

The Cultures of Congregations

July 6

Dear Ken,

I always look forward to receiving your newsletter on a particular week in November. Around Thanksgiving time the issue comes with a photo of the Pilgrim Family for the year. You've told me how important the Thanksgiving service at Mayflower Congregational is to you, to the congregation, and to the community. From surveying the bulletins you've sent, I'd have to agree that if somebody wanted to participate in a quintessential Thanksgiving Day celebration that resonates with the pilgrim story, Mayflower would be the place.

Don't think I'm poking fun at the Pilgrim Family, even if their costumes do make me smile. (I assume they perform this role in good humor, too, and smile at their own photo.) After all, St. Paul United Methodist Church where I go has an annual Possum Queen fund-raiser. Everybody votes for candidates from the Golden Age Center, usually women more than seventy years of age. The winner gets a crown made from a mylar balloon and carries a piece of fur that looks a lot like a dead squirrel. You can't knock it—the Possum Queen Festival raised $4,000 this year.

I suppose now you want to protest that at least the pilgrims have more to do with church than possums do (you're just jealous because your Thanksgiving offering wasn't anywhere near $4,000). But I want to suggest that to discern "church" means exactly to look at all this congregational craziness in all it signifies to its participants. In fact, I'm going even further to say that this zany array of symbols and events is a spring of theological imagination that can help us better understand not only what the church is, but also the reign of God to which the church points and even the incarnate God.

The congregations we have, wherever they are, are the only church we've got. This means that church practices can be found only in cultural forms with all their particularities and peculiarities. To ignore culture or to make it subservient to an essential, pure, or abstract ideal is tyrannical because it fails to acknowledge that the church is always situated among real people. Just as God is essentially personal and communicative, so practices of church are essentially embodied and enacted in communities. To grow in the knowledge and love of God is to seek God's continuing incarnation in the world. One place to look for God's incarnation is in the churches.

In order to enter into the concreteness of congregational life and see what is revealed there, we have to pay attention to the culture of the congregation. "Culture" is notoriously difficult to define. The concept certainly embraces artifacts that are observable expressions of culture, such as symbolic objects, documents, and buildings. It also needs to include patterns of behavior associated with those artifacts, particularly the languages and practices through which a congregation sustains and extends its traditions, as well as what these things mean to participants. Observable artifacts and practices express the basic assumptions and outlooks of participants, what they value and the ends toward which they are working. And that carries a definition still further toward what anthropologist Clifford Geertz called the "webs of significance" that hold all these artifacts, practices, and values together in a worldview that participants find meaningful. Their worldview is their picture of what they believe or trust to be ultimately true, "their most comprehensive ideas of order."

So far we have more or less five layers of culture—artifacts, practices, values, significance, and worldview. To these we ought to add other terms we use to try to name what is distinctive about a congregation, such as its *character*—the way it characteristically approaches decisions or responds to crises—and *ethos*—the norms for behavior and the values those norms express. We might even try the word *identity*—a kind of self-sameness over time that makes a congregation particularly itself.

If all these terms are shape-shifting and elastic, so much the more is the lingo coming from recent popular business literature, such as the claim that "organizational culture" is "the way we do things around here." The phrase is simple and agreeable. Yet a lot of authors and consultants seem all too eager to show how readily an "effective" leader can intervene and change the "corporate culture," as if it were only a matter of setting new dress codes or giving motivational speeches to the employees.

I do think pastoral and lay leaders of churches can bring about change in congregational culture, and I'll write to you more specifically about that. But too often leaders are ready to make changes without acknowledging or taking seriously the culture in which they work. They view symbols and practices as being entrenched and intransigent and think that they will be the ones finally to break free of their hold and take the congregation in a new direction. Then they wonder why no one is following.

"Rather than assume that the primary task of ministry is to alter the congregation," wrote Hopewell, "church leaders should make a prior commitment to understand the given nature of the object they propose to improve. Many strategies for operating upon local churches are uninformed about the cultural constitution of the parish; many schemes are themselves exponents of the culture they fancy they overcome."

To learn a congregation's culture is to honor the people whose lives it expresses. When the people know they are honored and appreciated, they are much better prepared for a critical and constructive engagement with their own culture. They are more able to see it in new ways and imagine fresh perspectives on church.

The culture of a congregation is as complex as our attempts at definition. To grasp it requires less a systematic theory of it than an immersion in it. You have to be there, and more than that, to be there with intention, paying attention.

I compare a congregation's culture to a plate of spaghetti. I take hold of one noodle, absolutely determined to get to the end of it, only to discover that it is all tangled up with other noodles such that the harder I pull the more the entire pile threatens to slide off into my lap. Meanwhile, I'm getting splattered with my own premature conclusions. I also know that even if I could disassemble the whole plate of spaghetti, what I would have would be individual, rapidly drying strands of dough and congealing sauce, which only made sense as spaghetti when tossed together afresh in the main dish.

Think, for example, of a congregation singing a hymn. This seemingly simple act is widely shared among traditions but has a particular form in each church tradition. Not only that, the hymn brings together the poetry of an author with the musical style of a composer and all the associations of the historical periods of their respective compositions. Moreover the actual singing of the hymn is

a product of the instrumental training of the accom-
panist, and a deliberate selection by the liturgist, and
a compromise between competing theological interests in the congregation, and an occasion for teasing
another parishioner about her voice, and a stimulus to
tears for someone whose dear grandfather was evoked
by the tune, and so on to countless other tangles.

All these things are true at the same time; they are all
going on at once. To know a congregation well is to know
at least some of these tangles and to appreciate their
inseparability. Maybe this is why I see so many pastors
smiling during a hymn.

You aren't surprised to know by now that I'm
not much for trying to systematize all this. A theory of a
cultural "system" might be intriguing for a while, but ultimately it would crumble under the constant waves of
complexity it was trying to sort out. A typology of church
cultures, for example, can help me see aspects of a congregation that I might otherwise miss. It might be helpful
to consider — in the categories of a 1980s Hartford
study — whether my congregation sees itself as a "sanctuary" or haven of faith in a troubled world, or as an
"activist" organization seeking social change. I learn from
exploring — in Carl Dudley and Sally Johnson's terms —
my congregation's "pilgrim" qualities as a church that
originally helped its immigrant constituency get accli-
mated to America, or its amazing resilience as a "survivor"
in the adversities of economic hard times. But the more
deeply I look, the more I see how a congregation shares in
elements of all the types, or at least more than one.

What is fascinating about congregational culture is not how it models a system or type, but how it
uniquely manifests ways of being church. Each congregation has similarities with others; each is also unique. To
paraphrase Denham Grierson, educator from Australia,

Each congregation is like every other congregation.
Some congregations are like some other congregations.
No congregation is like any other congregation.

Although congregations bear many similarities, no congregation has exactly the same history, mix of personalities, or community location as any other. To understand it requires delving into its uniqueness and particularity.

Seeing and understanding congregational culture requires conscious participant observation. Immersed though pastors and lay leaders are in the daily activities of a congregation, they also need to pay careful attention to the significance of what is going on around them. Most of us who are actively involved in congregations are participant-observers at one level or another; it's mainly a matter of bringing the role to greater self-consciousness and intentionality. Pastors are naturally well-situated for this stance, because both the pastoral and the participant-observer roles are liminal, standing on the threshold between outsider and insider status. Most pastors are never fully part of the congregation; by definition they have been set apart to preside over, preach to, counsel, and represent the people at the Lord's Table. In most cases the congregation was there before the pastor arrived and will continue long after the pastor is gone. The role of participant-observer similarly balances both detachment and involvement, perspective and immersion.

Participant observation is an art. It requires being fully part of whatever is going on, in such a way that one's presence does not disrupt or seriously alter the activity. It also requires a differentiated step of paying attention, noticing things, making note. The more I practice this art, the more I see and understand.

You already do this, as you know. You sit up front as the service is beginning, consciously or unconsciously noticing who is present and who is missing from the congregation. To practice participant observation may mean to notice which seats are always occupied by the same persons, but beyond that to note which groups of people seat themselves in which areas of the room, and then further to connect that with other relationships such as classes or governing bodies where people may know one another or wish to support one another.

Most regular participants are aware, say, that at the conclusion of the service, almost everyone files through a narrow door at the front right side of the sanctuary to get to the parlor for coffee and conversation. To practice participant observation may mean to notice that a visitor does not know where that narrow door leads, and that the pastor standing at that door is not only slowing the line down but forcing everyone to come past her in order to leave, and further that the parlor with its furniture given by one of the church's founding families is as sacred in its own way as the sanctuary itself.

Participant observation is a means of delving into "the imaginative life of the people, their stories, metaphors, allegories, myths, analogies, proverbs, and acknowledged paradoxes," as Grierson put it. It begins with what can be immediately observed and moves deeper into what is significant about what one sees and hears. It is a sensitive and active listening, a paying attention that allows one to sense more deeply the culture of which one is also inevitably a part. Participant observation of a congregation's culture is a doorway into its imaginative life. It is also a path into the resources of theological imagination.

Tom

Symbols and Narratives

July 8

Dear Ken,

Get yourself a fresh cup of coffee. I'd like to tell you a story from my life as a pastor. I think I remember it so vividly because it marks the moment I realized that I needed to learn my congregation's culture.

The day Harold dropped by the church office my nerves were already frayed by the repeated interruptions of the agenda I had set for myself when I came in that morning. I had completed about half the stewardship letter I was composing to go out over my signature endorsing the pledge drive when a slamming door jolted me out of my tattered swivel chair. It required no deep thought to guess what this was all about; and sure enough, when I stepped outside my study door, Jennifer, the secretary I had hired two months before, was not at her desk. In her place sat Mabel, the woman who had been church secretary for twenty years prior to the retirement reception given for her five years ago. I had been told upon my arrival the previous June that there was some question about whether Mabel had actually retired, but she was not on the payroll. She just came in every few days as a church member who now volunteered to do virtually anything.

That included her self-appointed task of orient-
ing my new secretary to all the ins and outs of this historic church. "Tom, I just can't find anything around here
anymore," she was stating to me in her firm maternal
tones, and I knew at once why the secretary had stomped
out and why I was going to be in hot water. "I was looking for the records of the committee to plan family nights,
and, well, I just can't find them anywhere. Someone must
have thrown it all away."

Her steady gaze was X-raying every twitch of
my face, and for good reason. One day the week before,
inspired by Jennifer's enthusiasm, I wore a T-shirt and
jeans for an office cleaning day. We took down the two
yellowed paint-by-numbers pictures on the wall, one of a
shepherd and one of a church building like the little
brown church in the vale, and put up some jazzy prints
of flowers and a cat in a window. We dug into the files.
You wouldn't believe what we found in there (yes, you
would) — multiple copies of musical programs from thirty years back, minutes of committees that no longer
existed, bank statements and even florist receipts from
the 1970s. I must have filled six garbage bags with this
junk. And one of the files might have been the one on
family nights, I couldn't really remember, though I could
picture some sheets run off on an old ditto machine with
stage directions and instructions for the ushers.

"Somebody was asking me yesterday," Mabel
was saying, "how to organize everybody for the family
variety show next month, and I thought I'd show them
how we've always done that. Haven't had one in years." I
swallowed hard, choking back words that would have
gone something like, "They'll never do a family show
again the way you did it in 1972," but I kept walking
toward the hallway. "Oh, I'm sure they'll figure out a
good way to do it," I called over my shoulder — still, as I
knew, the wrong thing to say.

As I stepped out of the office, here came Harold through the church door, puffing on his pipe and eyeing me with his usual dour look. In each hand he was gripping a large paper sack, and judging from his straining muscles, they contained something heavy. "Got some things to show you," he said in his deep gravelly voice. "Thought we could put these up in the sanctuary someplace." I knew Harold was a woodworker and I had heard that he had a project going, but I didn't know what might be in those sacks. I hadn't picked up a woodworking tool myself since seventh-grade shop class. Reaching into the sacks with his gnarled fingers, he lifted out first one and then the other of two matching pieces and set them against the wall.

"This is part of the decoration from the old altar rail," he explained, "the one we put in when we remodeled in the 1950s. Solid brass; I just built a wood frame for them. I like the new sanctuary look all right, but I hate to see this beautiful brass go to waste. There's all kinds of it down in the boiler room, where the old fixtures from the dining room are. I'll make some more pieces when I can, but I thought these would look nice up around the altar someplace."

The word "tacky" was ricocheting inside my brain. The brass was not exactly ugly; you could tell that it was supposed to represent a bunch of grapes on a vine. But whether it was art worthy of enshrinement was another matter. And Harold had not asked whether, but where, to place these objects in the sanctuary.

So I unlocked the chancel door and we walked out onto the platform. The renovation of the sanctuary had been completed during my predecessor's tenure in warm, polished woods and simple, subdued tones. Heavy brass abstracts were going to leap off the walls at anyone who dared look their way. But together Harold and I noticed a symmetry in the wall angles on each side of the platform that would allow the pieces to complement each other and be visible from the pews. He set the screws in the old plaster, and by noon the chunks of brass were hanging permanently. They were placed directly above the tops of the pulpit chairs in which the liturgist and I were seated each Sunday morning. Harold and his wife were there every Sunday, too, and for the next few weeks the first thing I would see when I plopped down in my pulpit chair for the organ prelude was Harold out there grinning at me like the cat that swallowed the canary.

This is what I meant by the spaghetti plate. This was only one hour out of one morning of a pastorate (with considerable masking of the actual people involved). Consider the density of information about that congregation's culture provided by this little scenario, and the questions it provokes. Let's take the artifacts, for example. The pastor is sitting in a tattered swivel chair in an office decorated with old paint-by-numbers pictures. Where did these objects come from, and what keeps them from being replaced? The files are stuffed with old documents; are they simply neglected, or functioning as a kind of archive? The brass is from the 1950s, the first of two overhauls to sanctuary decor in fewer than thirty years. What causes this congregation to struggle so hard for appropriate symbols? Is it just a change of tastes between generations? What keeps the people from throwing away these artifacts while nonetheless storing them in a dark, dirty, mildewed space in the basement?

Or look at the behaviors and practices. What is stirring the pastor to write a fund-raising letter, to clean out the church files, and to stand by while Harold makes the arbitrary decision to add significant artifacts to the worship space? Is there some group that normally weighs (or fights about) such decisions first? Why didn't Mabel's retirement ceremony "take"? What authorizes her to rummage through the church office and tell Jennifer how to do her job?

Our questions push us to examine basic assumptions and values as well. What is so important about family night? Is this a family church, or did it used to be family-oriented and isn't sure how to cope with an influx of single yuppies who like cat posters? What gives long-time members like Harold and Mabel so much clout?

Finally we find ourselves wanting to know more about the "webs of significance" that hold all this together and the worldview reflected in these artifacts, behaviors, and assumptions. What is the church for, in the eyes of its participants? How does their congregational culture mirror the kind of world for which they hope? Who is God to them, and what is God calling them to do?

These layers of questions are the field for participant observation and the stuff of theological imagination. I am convinced that if pastoral and lay leaders will take time to pay deep attention to such questions, they will be rewarded with a vastly enriched understanding of their congregation and the way it particularly expresses its faith.

One way to begin is by examining a congregation's symbolic objects. Like the brass, they signify in multiple dimensions, and the complex narrative lines of congregational life often wind around them. Harold's brass pieces represented grapes and vines, an evocation of biblical images of fruitfulness and communion. They were from a particular era of the congregation's history when it was growing rapidly and church attendance was high. The surrounding city and nation were in the flush of rising income and a sense of nobility that reinforced American society's belief in its special providential status after World War II. Everyone looking at the objects would not know all those layers, yet all attach to the objects and are sustained in some part of the collective memory.

Hopewell concluded from studying the stories of congregations that narrative has a "fundamental relationship [with] congregational life." He suggested three ways in which this is true. First, "the congregation's self-perception is primarily narrative in form." Nobody could explain the brass pieces without telling the whole story of the successive church renovations. When I asked people about Mabel, trying to learn more about how she was perceived, I got more stories than I could take in. Whenever I suggested a new idea, I needed to be prepared to hear stories through which participants would try to connect what I was proposing with their known experience as a storied community. This takes a lot of patience; how many times do I have to hear about how many neat kids were in the youth group thirty years ago? But by listening I could honor and affirm "the congregation's self-perception."

Second, "The congregation's communication among its members is primarily by story." I have discovered that a simple question posed to a participant — "How did you happen to become a member of this congregation?" — can evoke a story of twenty minutes' duration. I can't tell my own story without telling about other people and events, which leads to other intertwining narratives, which all taken together are what bind a congregation into a whole. Moreover, participants make sense of people and events by telling stories. Is this gossip? Yes, sometimes warm and funny, sometimes hurtful and hateful, but always revealing of what sense people are making. Chatter about a teen pregnancy, a faulty electrical repair, or an accident with the church van may be sympathetic or may degenerate into blame and exclusion. In any case it signals ways in which participants are trying to make sense of what happened and to weave it into the continuing narrative structure of their congregation's culture.

Third and most elusively, Hopewell proposed that "by its own congregating, the congregation participates in narrative structures of the world's societies." That is, congregations draw on "the treasury of symbolic forms" that has been built up over generations by human groups trying to make sense of the world and express their faith. A congregation's stories are often mythic in dimension, signifying what is most profoundly true for this group of people. In this sense congregants share in the struggle for myth that continues in the wider culture. What made the stories of packed sanctuaries and overflowing youth choir rehearsals mythic for that old city church? They were foundational to its sense of worth and power; they were expressive of the congregation's struggle to accommodate rapid change in the city's landscape.

I have come to think of congregational narrative as a dense fabric made up of many strands of varied colors and textures. Some of the strands are individual stories of how a person found this congregation, what was going on in her life at the time, and how events in her family have affected church relationships. Some of the yarns are collective in nature, events that everyone who was there would remember—the altar curtain falling on the pastor as he blessed the offering plates, the little girl clinging to her mother's legs as she served the communion bread, the members from the mental retardation center shouting the Lord's Prayer at the top of their lungs.

Some thicker strands are mythic in quality. Here are some words from First Korean United Methodist Church in Chicago, for example:

> We purchased a Jewish synagogue and are using it for our church building. The beautiful sanctuary stained-glass windows are decorated with Jewish symbols. A few years ago, we decorated the remaining

windows in the sanctuary with Jesus' image as the good shepherd in stained glass. The sanctuary seems to be the most wondrous place to worship God. It is also a very meaningful place to signify our journey from the Hebrew tradition and the Protestant tradition, finally to that of the Korean-American.

These are the larger narratives that most fundamentally tell a particular congregation who they are and what sense their journey makes in the world.

Yet another strand, woven in and through the others, often hard to detect or seen only in retrospect, is gospel narrative itself—signs of God's reign right here in this church. "Every congregation," wrote theologian Lewis Mudge,

> continues the biblical story through its own stories. These contemporary extensions of the biblical style and plot in the congregation's own history become the carriers of the faith community's identity. Such continuations of the biblical story highlight significant events which have had a certain transforming and binding power for those who participated in them . . . Above all, such narratives recount stories of faith.

Central to "biblical style" is to look for signs of who in the name of God these people think they are. Foster and Brelsford were almost overwhelmed by the complexity of the stories they were hearing. All three congregations they studied had, over time, come to include more than one ethnic and cultural group, a phenomenon in itself all too rare in American Protestantism. Yet they had arrived at this in entirely unique ways.

Finally the research team settled on a way of grasping this complexity without diminishing it. They identified signs around which stories clustered. The signs enabled them to establish "an interpretative trajectory" for understanding other stories, and to weave multiple stories together into a thematic pattern. This included what was unspoken as well, the gaps and silences, "stories that had been repressed or shoved to the margins of the corporate consciousness." Having identified the signs, the team could then explore their significance in dialogue with members.

Some of the signs were recurring expressions; in one church, people often used the phrase "We are family," or said about a new project, "We just do it." These words reflected and reinforced their fundamental outlook of not allowing problems to dissuade them from what they felt called to do. Some of the signs were visual or physical in nature; in one church, the sanctuary's round shape with a wide altar rail around a central communion table signified the inclusion of all peoples. A reading of the parable of the messianic banquet was vivid there.

Signs thus also mirror biblical images. I've heard a lot of teasing over the years about how all that Methodists need to start a new congregation is a coffee pot and all that Baptists need is a barbecue pit. There is truth here. I'm amazed how often people will describe a common reverie as they sit in the sanctuary, smelling the food as it warms in the kitchen below and anticipating the fellowship of the table after worship. They are in reverie with the smells, tastes, sights, spaces, and people through which they struggle to make sense of their lives. They are revisiting pain and alienation; they are remembering warmth and affirmation.

In congregations that anticipate a messianic banquet and hope to be signs of human well-being and justice, and that enact a simple meal of bread and juice to remember and renew God's love and reconciliation, such

reveries are not merely incidental. They are signals insep-
arably woven together with the central signs that remind
a congregation of its identity and purpose.

Tom

Reflections

Congregations: Community and Culture

Talk of food and the church is a distinct
reminder of the connection among personal reverie, congregational culture, and church practices. Melvin
Williams's detailed description of the kitchen in
Community in a Black Pentecostal Church provides a fine
example.

> The kitchen is a room on the first floor of the build-
> ing with two windows with counters opening onto
> the main hallway. One is used to serve take-out items
> when the kitchen is overcrowded and the entrance to
> it is blocked. It is also used by the cooks and wait-
> resses to observe who is going into the church and to
> greet and delay those whom they choose. The other
> window is used for hat checking as well as for the
> sale of small confections during large meetings. . . .
>   When the kitchen is open, many members
> spend most of their worship time there and listen to
> services through a loudspeaker. If something is sig-
> naled (a favorite speaker is introduced, a large emo-
> tional "shout" occurs, or a preacher begins to over-
> whelm), aprons fly off and patrons rush upstairs to
> witness, often neglecting to pay for their food. The
> kitchen is the "crossroads of the state." All are seen

here at one time or another. . . . Some spend more time here than in the regular worship services, and many flock here during the "change of services" when offerings are being taken. Some get up and march around to the offering table and give, and then, tired of sitting through the long services, go to the kitchen to socialize and refill. The kitchen is first to open and last to close.

The more Williams hung out around not only the kitchen, but many other activities of this congregation, the more he realized that "food is a pervasive theme in the conceptual framework of the membership." He heard countless expressions, such as a description of active fellow members as "so sweet that honey is falling out of their mouths," or as having a "butter-mouthed tongue." A "sweet dumpling" or a "pumpkin pie" described someone who was amenable to a program suggestion, while a "sour peach" was a disagreeable sister. Only the strongest members could digest "strong meat" or "black-eyed peas at night."

Was this just some sort of peculiar folk heritage, a cute eccentricity of this little congregation of an old neighborhood in Pittsburgh? When he put food together with other language about land and animals, and watched the tight bonds among church members, Williams decided not. What he was seeing, he concluded, was a community comprising families who had migrated from the rural South looking for industrial jobs in 1940s Pittsburgh. Their language and their kitchen affirmed their roots, providing a way for displaced people to stay connected with land and place. In a larger society that usually rejected them and in which they could get only the most menial jobs, the church provided a space for being a community of rest, affirmation, dignity, and hope.

What Williams learned from these observations has made me reconsider what I have often dismissed as trivial or ridiculous in congregations I know. What people are saying or doing, their artifacts and practices, are not accidental or incidental. There are reasons for them. People express what is most meaningful in their lives through their culture.

One constructive way to think about congregations is their capacity for providing what Mudge called a "social space" for making community. I imagine this space in three concentric circles. The innermost is the fellowship of participants in the congregation who by their interactions over time build up a web of relationships and a culture of myth and meaning that binds them together. This community evokes loyalty, love, and care, even as it stirs anger and conflict. It also generates the stories, symbols, rituals, language, and outlooks that participants come to share and to recognize as part of a common culture.

The next circle is the larger neighborhood and network of relationships and activities with which the congregation, individually and collectively, is intertwined. This larger community also has its own cultural consistency embodied in story and symbol, as well as institutions such as schools, libraries, arts centers, government agencies, hospitals, and businesses with which a congregation has variable levels of engagement. A congregation both reflects this neighborhood culture and is a catalytic or transformative element within it.

The third, broadest circle is the social space of the larger society and global human community. A congregation shares in cultural elements of that greater community, not only through symbols such as flags or songs, but also through common questions and struggles over appropriate values and ends. In the social space of a congregation one rightly expects to hear of compassion for people suffering from hunger or natural disaster, and of wrestling with values of sexuality, marriage, children, and family. As the larger national and world community searches for "symbols capable of binding communities together and sustaining a moral vision of the universe," in Mudge's words, I anticipate seeing that search exemplified in some ways in a congregation.

Having described these circles, though, already I am dissatisfied with the image. At the very least these circles must be porous because there is much flowing back and forth between congregation, neighborhood, national and world community. These cannot be rigid boundaries — no matter how hard a particular congregation might try to make them so. The very materials with which a congregation builds up its culture are more widely shared in any case. As Mudge put it,

> A congregation, living a story which embodies its own identity, takes on certain signifying elements of the society and culture around it. Forms of governance, works of art and architecture, perspectives related to class, race and gender, newspaper stories used as sermon illustrations: these are the sorts of things that are appropriated into the fabric of ecclesial existence.

Given this constant cultural borrowing and interacting, I'd be closer to the reality if I could imagine these circles in three dimensions and in motion, with all three moving and flowing into and out of one another while still being distinct.

Big Bethel is one of the oldest congregations in Atlanta, an African Methodist Episcopal church that sits on a corner of Auburn Avenue near downtown. "Sweet Auburn" is the historic center of black culture in Atlanta, home of the Royal Peacock jazz lounge, Ebenezer Baptist Church, and the Martin Luther King, Jr., grave and museum, and a library of African American literatures.

Pastors of Big Bethel have always been public figures in Atlanta and its lay members often prominent in business, education, and government. Yet its membership also represents a wide diversity of social class within the black community.

One time I led a research team in meeting with a small group of laity to ask them to tell stories of their church, what it means to them and what they value most there. It quickly became apparent that their church stories could not be disentangled from neighborhood stories, that their narrative as a congregation was inseparable from the narrative of black folks in Atlanta, in Georgia and the deep South, and in the United States as a whole.

Take the sanctuary, for example. Congregants associate their pulpit not only with the tenure of their well-known preachers over the years. In their eye of memory they also see U.S. presidents standing there. They see political meetings held in the sanctuary to plan strategy for civil rights. Their announcement time includes not just ice cream in the fellowship hall, but also someone to see if you are looking for a job, or to talk to if you are having family problems.

One of the visually striking aspects of Big Bethel is the arrangement of the sanctuary. It is a rectangular room definitely longer one way than the other, but the platform and choir loft are along one of the long walls with the pews and balcony curved around in an arc. Instead of meeting longways, with focus on a high altar at a narrow front wall, Big Bethel members sit in these broad pews facing the wide wall. Around the platform is a sweeping altar rail, to which members process to give their tithes or to kneel for Communion. At prayer time dozens of people press forward into the altar rail to join hands and pray together at the pastor's leading.

The sense of gathering is palpable at Big Bethel. Clearly this is a space in which people from all walks of life and from many different Atlanta neighborhoods can come together at the rail. In this space six generations of African Americans have found ways to take leadership, to address community needs, and to form an identity as a people seeking rights of participation in a larger society that has often excluded them. Coming to the rail is an act of freedom and affirmation, a statement that confirms one's dignity and solidarity with others.

Big Bethel has a large continuing community of church participants, some more formally members and some not. Though its membership is widely dispersed across the metropolitan area, the church is inseparable from its neighborhood—as one member put it, "Auburn Avenue makes Big Bethel Big Bethel . . . [we] have not forgotten where [we] are." And Big Bethel is also a catalyst for engagement with larger social issues of race and class in American society. All three of these "circles" are permeable, in motion and interactive at the same time in the "social space" of this church.

The creating of social space is no trivial task in the culture of privacy and consumerism in which we live. Yet as world societies contend with increasingly pressing issues of the natural environment, economic development, and conflict among ethnic groups, the work of making holistic communities becomes increasingly urgent. In this task, with their stock of symbol and myth, loyalty and commitment, congregations have the capacity for a catalytic role. As Hopewell stated it,

> The local church is a microcosm of human culture, an immediate instance of the world's symbolic imagination. . . . The worldwide toil to knit a human community out of disparate motives and symbols occurs in specific instance in the local church; the congregation . . . is an immediate microcosm of all society's attempts to associate.

Thus we must both pay more acute attention to the social space of our congregations and be more watchful about the kind of community catalyst congregations can be. This has come more readily, perhaps, to congregations such as the African American churches I have been describing, whose constituencies have been continually at risk or displaced in the larger society. Because they have been pushed to the margins, African Americans have had more incentive to learn their stories, to celebrate their symbols, and to connect their lives intimately with the larger gospel story of reconciliation and freedom. White churches whose constituencies have ready access to neighborhood, regional, and national institutions have had less incentive to be aware of their own congregation's way of being community. They have had less cause to tell their stories and less motive for imagining how their congregational narrative expresses a gospel narrative.

The days of any group living in an assumed culture are past, however. The churches cannot look to the dominant commercial culture to provide an accurate reflection of Christian symbols, or expect to see gospel narratives of healing and reconciliation acted out naturally in their social institutions. Congregations need to be far more deliberate about understanding the depth and power of their own culture as well as its capacity to help transform larger communities. Mudge again:

> Churches are already meeting places of many interests and cultures . . . they can provide places where some of the needed practical reasoning about the good for humanity can go on. They can help create spaces in human society where larger, more visionary questions about the purpose of human life can be asked.

So is the Pilgrim Family class-bound and questionably related to historical fact? Is the Possum Queen Festival a laughable way to be church? Yes. Our congregational forms use elements of our cultures, becoming incarnate and thus limited, and even downright funny—better to laugh than to cry. Yet these are the only materials we have for being church, and we use them in the hope that they might be signs of something greater: God's reign of well-being and justice, the human community made whole.

The Framework of Imagining: Time, Space, and the Sense of Place

The Time of Our Lives

July 15

Dear Ken,

I've asked you to share my trust that in exploring their own cultures, congregations will be led to new
insights into their ministry and mission. But I don't propose this only as a way to strengthen a congregation's
self-image of vitality. If congregations in their practices
are striving to bear witness to Good News for the whole
world, then we must consider how they might be catalysts for transformation of the larger society as well. This
leads me to suggest how congregations can reflect on the
basic dimensions that frame the worldview of the wider
culture within which they live and work. This will mean
examining the perceptions of time, space, and the sense
of place through which we locate ourselves and our purposes in the world.

Congregations in many ways mirror the com-
mon framework. But they can also reflect on it critically
through their practices of worship, fellowship, and service. Congregations make a space in which to remember

and create symbols and rituals that build up human community, itself an enormous contribution to a busy and distracted society. Congregations are uniquely poised to consider Mudge's broadest sphere of social space, "larger, more visionary questions about the purpose of human life."

This is not as abstract as it may sound at first. Our assumptions about time and space are obvious in how we organize our work and build our buildings, though we may not think about them very much. We largely take the world of nature for granted as the "natural" backdrop for our activities and rarely throw a glance at what gives us a sense of place, even though our lives are self-evidently dependent on these settings. Yet attending to these basic dimensions of understanding can reveal both how deeply imbedded in them we are and the possibilities for transforming them as well.

I'd like to describe what I mean by beginning with the dimension of time. As you well know and constantly remind me, I do not wear a watch. I had one up through young adulthood, but about twenty years ago it broke and I never replaced it. Since I quit wearing a watch I have learned a lot about time. For one thing, I've learned that not all minutes are identical. They may be measurably the same, but some minutes are longer than others. The forty-five minutes sitting in a traffic jam on the Atlanta interstate perimeter are an eternity compared with the forty-five minutes that fly past in a phone call with my sister in England. The hands on the office wall clock barely seem to move as I wait for my doctor's appointment scheduled to begin thirty minutes ago; but when the last ten minutes of a Georgia Tech basketball game take thirty minutes to play because the score is so close and every basket counts, I don't even notice the time. I never seem to have time enough to buy that card for the surprise birthday party, but at the moment I blurt out to my friend that I'll see him at the party tonight—the party that was supposed to be a surprise for him—time freezes in its tracks.

In other words, time is elastic. It is not simply a linear sequence; it also stretches into moments of fullness. I've found this particularly true in worship. One of my pastors used to begin the pastoral prayer with the words "Let us pray," and then would wait so long to begin speaking that I peeked to see if he had fallen asleep or passed out. Yet that silence stretched the congregation not only across linear time but into a depth of presence. Likewise with the occasional anthem or sermon or moment of prayer kneeling at the altar rail—time as we usually count it sometimes gives way to time as being.

Not wearing a watch has forced me to pay attention in a way I never did before. I find myself being more attentive to the rhythm of time in a particular setting. Every group has its own pace for moving its work forward. I find myself listening carefully for the hang-ups, the sloughs, the turning points, the rise of consensus, the moments of new insight and breakthrough.

Thus one of the most ordinary questions of our daily lives seems to have multiple dimensions. What time is it, and by what kind of measure, and from what perspective? Edward T. Hall identified nine different kinds of time that are constantly interactive in human life. For instance, "biological time" marks such phenomena as the aging process, my struggle to adjust my "body clock" after an overseas plane trip, or a woman's menstrual cycle. "Sync time" describes the "beat" or rhythm unique to a culture or even a city or town. "Physical time" is measured in the movements of sun, moon, and planets.

After years of ethnographic work, Hall decided that world cultures organize time in at least two fundamental ways. In "polychronic" cultures, many things are always going on at once and time is multiple and intangible. "P-time" emphasizes relationships, transactions among people, and complex networks of communication. Offices are often small and cluttered with stacks of paper; the real business is conducted in more communal spaces where all clients or customers are waited on at once and have the sense of participating together. Time is never solid or firm.

I found in a trip to East Africa, for example, that I would be invited to a party at "eight for eight-thirty." I soon discovered that if I arrived at eight, I would find the hosts not yet even dressed; if I arrived at eight-thirty I'd be the first one there; if I came around nine I'd probably find some people gathering; and if I was there by nine-thirty, the festivities would be warming up. In other words, "eight for eight-thirty" told me that sometime around sunset—since equatorial African days and nights are all pretty much the same length—I should remember that there's a party, then think about what I might wear, then take care of some phone calls, then get dressed, and then get there later on.

Polychronic cultures are typical of much of Africa, Latin America, southern Europe, and the Middle East, in Hall's account. North American and northern European cultures predominantly tend toward monochronic time. "M-time" is divided into discrete, measurable units, and distinct activities are allocated to each time block. Each individual person keeps a calendar, in many cases a published book with days lined off into hour, half-hour, or quarter-hour blocks. Attorneys, business consultants, and therapists keep time logs as finely detailed as six-minute intervals in order to record "billable hours." Appointments or meetings in most organizations are limited to one piece of business or an agenda of items of which participants typically know in advance. Since time designated by the clock (which is set according to scientific standards based on Greenwich mean time) is what allows us to meet in the same place at the same time, it behooves one to be on time and not have a reputation for being late.

"M-time" generates metaphors predicated on time as scarce commodity. Nothing is worse in this culture than to "waste" time, or to have to "kill" it. We either "use" time or "lose" it. Time "marches" on, so you'd better develop a time "line" for your project because time is "running out" and dallying now will make for a time "crunch" later. If I'm alert I can "save" time, "make" time, or even "make good time," but often I just don't "have" time.

Time as commodity organizes life for the commercial culture that dominates the West and increasingly much of the rest of the world. In America, time is money and productivity; one must have something to show for one's time. But for most Americans time is not only linear, the chronology of our lives laid out along a line of hours, days, weeks, months, and years. Time moves on and ever upward in the ascent of progress. The chronologies of our individual and institutional lives must depict a continuous journey toward ever-higher goals, upward mobility, and never-ending growth.

Americans are compulsive consumers of time. Complaining that we never have enough time, we race from one activity to the next. We buy the latest technology to help us complete tasks more quickly so that we can fill that time with more productive activities. After all, if our lives were not a noticeable improvement over our parents' lives, and their parents' lives—in fact, if the current era were not clearly the most advanced in human history—then the obsessions of our age would have no point. Time is the line we grip in the hope of being carried to happiness, and the line on which our dominant commercial culture hangs every evidence of its most precious totem—progress.

We work, study, play, write, drive, sleep, and eat under the watchful faces of our clocks. We also may pray, sing, and preach under them. Recently I was strolling down the sidewalk of a little mountain town in North Carolina on a sunny Saturday afternoon. I noticed that the wooden double doors of the frame Presbyterian church were standing open. I'd always wanted to see inside this structure, built in the 1870s, so I strode up the steps and into the sanctuary. It was still, no sound but the creak of floorboards under my feet. The red carpet, curved wooden pews, pulpit centering a high platform, white plaster walls, and elegant Tiffany stained-glass windows all evoked the years of worship in that place. Then in the quiet I became aware of a repeated sound—tick, tock, tick, tock. There on the wall of the nave hung a wind-up pendulum clock keeping time for the congregation.

In an M-time culture, even at worship we often want to know what hour and minute it is, how much time has elapsed and how much remains, lest we "spend" too much time in the activity of praise. We have a mission to fulfill, after all, and we must be about it.

In short, instead of trying to moderate the dominance of M-time in our commercial culture, churches often have advocated it as the normative framework for the moral life. Well-ordered and managed time is essential to the Protestant ethic, which teaches that every individual has a vocation for which he or she is responsible and through which he or she will "work out" his or her own salvation. For churches composed of full participants in the market economy—particularly churches of northern European heritage—any questioning of M-time is tantamount to sin.

For people who have been denied the benefits of this economy, or who have serious questions about it, M-time has not been so compelling. Churches of African American heritage, for example, organize time in a much more polychronic style. Worship may last several hours. Devout members are likely to spend almost all of a Sunday at church. But of course, for people continually faced with racism, church has been home, a place to go when there is "no other helper." The church is not a discrete unit apart from daily society that is allocated a distinct length of time and no more. The church is the community, and because it is community it is likely to have many activities going on at once all day long, from meals to entertainment to employment services and credit unions to political addresses and appeals. White folks do all this stuff in specialized institutions outside the church to which they have ready access, traditionally expecting to find (white) Christians punctually carrying out their honest work at the bank, insurance office, or store. For blacks, such distinctions have generally not held.

Women of whatever ethnicity also have lived in perennial tension with M-time. Their lives are typically more polychronic. Women's experience is constituted not solely by rationalized, managed time, but also by biological rhythms of menstruation and, for many, pregnancy and childbirth. While men organize their lives primarily around the achievement of tasks, "women's lives center on networks of people and their relations with people," in Hall's words. When a husband accepts a company promotion that entails a move to another city, the wife typically bears the emotional burden of breaking off friendships.

In my pastoral experience, it has most often been women who initiated contact with the church and sought membership, among other things as a way of establishing new relationships for themselves and their families. Many times I have observed men eager to leave the church building and get on to another activity while women lingered in conversation. In many congregations the female participants outnumber the male by as much as four to one, and as a male pastor I was regularly aware of working with groups—committees, classes, prayer and study cells—that were predominantly female.

What this pattern signals is that congregations, while often adhering to the M-time that controls American commercial culture, have also provided ways of keeping in perspective the social organization that M-time imposes. I enjoyed your church newsletter recently in which you identified three calendars that operate in your church. The secular "Gregorian" calendar that governs much of our institutional and personal lives in Western societies runs from what we call "January" to what we call "December." After that we celebrate what we call a "new year," and commercial culture hypes it as if it were the only such ritual in the world, even though there are many calendars and many new years in various cultures (Chinese, Jewish, Islamic, and so on).

You pointed out that your church also has a "fiscal" year that runs from July 1 to June 30, which corresponds more to a kind of "program year" for the congregation's activities. The church "closes the books" and "takes stock" of its finances at a time of relatively low activity when large expenditures are complete.

It's interesting to me how much this parallels another calendar that dominates church life, namely, the "school" pattern. A congregation's programs tend to kick off with a "rally day" in September when schools and universities begin the academic year. Culminating events such as Sunday school promotions and church membership confirmations fall nearer the end of the "school" year in April or May, thus giving the feel of "graduation." Summer then becomes a special "time out of time" when the academic clock is not running and children go to camp, families take vacations, and many church members take a few weeks or months off from attending worship.

To this you added the "liturgical" calendar that traces the "Christian year" from Advent through

Pentecost, a cyclical recounting of the Jesus narrative and the formation of church. Dates for this calendar are a mystery to many church participants. One first has to figure out when Easter is, the one remaining Christian festival that depends on sun and moon. Most people look it up in a printed church calendar instead of calculating it for themselves. In dominant M-time culture we have no reason to note the moon's phases other than noticing when the full moon is unmistakably bright.

Many other "calendars" are "keeping time" in the congregation as well. A local community often celebrates events in an annual cycle that shapes congregational life. A church in Oceana County, Michigan, can hardly ignore the Asparagus Festival that comes around every June. The Spoleto Music Festival spanning the period from April through June in Charleston, South Carolina, involves many congregations as concert venues and as choral participants. Conversely, for many communities a church's own celebrations are important events in town life. Homecoming Sunday and the pastor's anniversary Sunday are occasions for large gatherings, dinner on the grounds, concerts, and special services.

The seasonal calendar has a marked effect on churches located in Florida or along the Gulf Coast as the snowbirds flock in in the winter months, or on churches in the Blue Ridge Mountains as towns multiply tenfold in population for the summer. Numerous camp-meetings, chautauquas, retreat centers, and camping facilities are active in summer months as well, often affecting the life of surrounding congregations.

Thus churches are polychronic in nature; that is, in congregational life we experience many calendars and many senses of time. This confuses some people, and I have met purists on all sides, some who want the church to "operate like a business" on one definite January-to-December calendar, and some who want a church separate from the world and running strictly on its own liturgical time, the time of forming people in the Christian story. But the fact is that an incarnate church, a people of God living through institutional forms in certain locations in particular societies, is going to have multiple calendars.

The compelling incarnational question is how to sanctify time, in my colleague Don Saliers's terms. The liturgical calendar is a great help to this, as a way to "keep time with Jesus . . . opening the treasury of who Jesus is and what he proclaims." Marking time in the Christian year is a "discipline" that enables us "to understand and to reorder our emotions, desires, and intentions" by the pattern of Jesus' life, death, and resurrection. We experience a "rhythm of incarnation" as we are shaped by Advent's promise and expectation, Lent's introspection and discipleship, Easter's joy, and Pentecost's vitality and giftedness.

This sanctification of time, though, is inseparable from the rhythms of our life narratives (and wouldn't be very sanctifying if it were separate). I think of the life cycle of church members—the teenage girl sitting quietly through youth group wondering what her first period means for her body, the new retiree staring out the window all through the worship service puzzled about what to do with his leisure, the newlywed couple holding hands at coffee hour as people begin to receive them as a pair. An incarnate sense of God's time "redeems the time" appropriately for people at whatever point they are in their unfolding stories.

The disciplined rhythm of Christian seasons provides a pattern for sensing what time it is in our lives. "Because all of us continue to undergo the changes of life—growth, suffering, passages of various kinds, and death—the liturgical year is never quite the same each time we move through it," as Saliers put it. Attention to the dispositions of following Jesus' life and ministry opens insight into what is coming to fruition, what is decisive, what needs to change in our own lives. This is the transformative sense of time to which the gospel calls us.

Tom

Reflections

Discerning the Time

In a culture of individualism we grow accustomed to thinking of our personal lives as distinct narratives. We assume the freedom to make autonomous choices (an assumption that would seem bizarre and desperate in most human cultures through history). What we have much greater difficulty conceiving is our collective narratives as congregations. The liturgical year is a kind of corporate narrative, to be sure, that pulls us individually into a pattern shared widely among churches. But how do we go about discerning the time for us as a local collective entity, a congregation that continues "over time"? What time is it in our congregation?

These questions call us to attend more carefully to the narratives of our congregations. We need to know our own stories as corporate communities that reach across generations and endure through continually changing social conditions. We need to probe the depths of memory and meaning to find the ligaments of loyalty and hope that bind us together, and the signs that point toward decisions and directions for the future. I am not calling for self-absorption or coziness as a turning inward, as if we were locking the doors, pulling the chairs up to the fireplace, and telling stories about the good old days. I am advocating a healthy and wise self-knowledge that can free us from the compulsions of contemporary-mindedness and help us make timely responses to God's purposes for the world.

This collective effort is both provoked and deepened by scriptural language for time. Many biblical references to time use the Greek term *chronos*, the root of English words like chronology. This was a term signifying endurance or duration, the ordinary time of daily living. When Jesus encountered the man lying by the Pool of Bethzatha, Jesus knew intuitively that he had been there "a long time," and indeed the gospel writer supplies the information that the man had been ill for thirty-eight years (John 5:6).

A contrasting word for time, and sense of time, appears right from the start of Mark's account. What Mark reports as Jesus' first sermon begins with the words, "The time is fulfilled" (Mark 1:15). Here the Greek word is *kairos*. This is a rich and layered term, meaning a decisive moment, a turning point, a time of fruition and fulfillment when something that has been moving into place is at the point of coming to pass. Matthew uses *kairos* as the term to describe the harvest-time when the grain is full and weeds can be separated from the crop (Matt. 13:30), or the precise moment when grapes of the vineyard are ready for picking to make the best wine (Matt. 21:34). Or one thinks of Paul's image of all creation as a pregnant woman, crying in labor pains as the time of birth at last arrives, and "the sufferings of this present time" give way to glory (Rom. 8:18).

Luke shows Jesus pondering how it is that people can study the clouds for signs of rain or the winds to expect a hot day, but still can miss how "to interpret the present time" (Luke 12:56). Luke has Jesus shedding tears over Jerusalem for the city's failure to recognize the moment it has been waiting for all these years, the time fulfilled, the "decisive point of time," the day of God's visitation, its *kairos* (Luke 19:44).

The time has come, New Testament letters declare, for followers of Christ to live in a new age, as if the new time is here. "Be careful then how you live," Ephesians admonishes, "not as unwise people but as wise, making the most of the time, because the days are evil." Or as the Jerusalem Bible has it in its usual pithy manner, "This may be a wicked age, but your lives should redeem it" (Eph. 5:15-16).

This last, more ethical, usage of *kairos* evokes its sense in ancient Greek rhetoric as the appropriate or propitious time, the moment of fit. Anyone who has studied and practiced rhetoric knows that an excellent speaker or leader can sense the right time for the compelling word, the clinching argument, the decisive action, that will make a difference. But it also must be a word that is proportional to the situation, fitting or merited in a particular circumstance.

Kairos, then, must be carefully discerned. Everybody seems to be using the word "discernment" these days and I don't mean to fall back on a buzzword. When I first learned this word, I thought it applied mainly to social occasions. To say a person had "discerning taste" meant that she or he knew just what to wear or how to decorate a table for a cocktail party. A person of "discernment" I took to be somewhat above the rest of us, able to make distinctions about appropriateness that I might find snobby.

But recently I've been considering the root of this word more deeply. To discern means "to separate" or "to discriminate." If I discern a bird in a tree I am visually separating it from the blue of sky and green of branches. Discernment is the noting and distinguishing of differences. The word derives from the action of sifting, getting the lumps out of the flour or the wheat out of the chaff. Discernment captures the attentiveness needed to see or distinguish the *kairos*, to read the signs of the times.

One problem I have with discernment, though, is the dilemma of being an astute observer who is discriminating in word and deed without becoming overparticular in my insistence on everything being "just right." How do I keep discernment from becoming merely a means of limiting and controlling my responsibilities? Those Pharisees who insisted on tithing even the herbs growing on the windowsill were only trying to be faithful, after all (Matt. 23:23). Jesus accused them of ignoring larger proportionalities of justice, surely a fitting accusation, though reviewing my own life I find it easy to see how these devout people had gotten themselves into that position.

The gospel often does not seem just or fair in the usual sense. There is no way those workers who arrived at 5:00 p.m. deserved the same wage as the ones who came at 9:00 a.m., even if it was exactly what the boss promised (Matt. 20:1-16). Where are the boundaries of proportionality if everybody on the streets gets invited to the banquet? (Luke 14:15-24).

Indeed the gospel accounts suggest that there are times—a *kairos*—for throwing off all sense of proportion for words and deeds appropriate to some vaster reality. A woman pours an entire bottle of ointment over Jesus' head (Mark 14:3-9). Five thousand people are fed and satisfied from five loaves and two fish (Mark 6:30-44). When the younger son who has squandered his inheritance returns home, the father welcomes him back with abundance so lavish it merits the term "prodigal" (Luke 15:11-32).

So maybe there is a time for us to give the budget surplus to the poor, not just roll it over into the building fund. Maybe there is a time for our congregation to cancel the pledge campaign and ask people to let the Spirit guide their giving. Maybe there is a time to cease all program and committee work for six months and study the scriptures together. I don't know exactly what is required, and that is precisely where discernment comes in.

A few years ago I consulted with a predominantly white church in the affluent suburbs of Atlanta. When the lay leader first called me, I assumed that he was asking me to lead a planning process. But it turned out that a long-range planning committee was already in place and had done its homework. They had collected pages of demographic data, economic and real estate forecasts, and charts depicting the past growth and current plateau in their congregation's attendance. They were worried, though. Why wasn't their church growing like some of the neighboring congregations? Why did the congregation seem grumpy and divided? They had clear goals to propose. Their fear was that the people would be too demoralized to act on them.

We met one evening to try a different approach. Each person told a story of how he or she happened to become a member and a story that would say something about the congregation's distinctive character. We heard about the time Bill had been laid off at Lockheed and members of the church gave him daily phone calls of support and helped the family out with fees for his kids' activities. We heard about youth recruiting school friends to help with a Habitat for Humanity project. We heard about Julie taking the initiative to start a new group for single moms. We made a list of what people valued most about this congregation.

The group then described in a word or phrase what the community around the church was like. Words came fast and furious: transient, affluent, divorce, single parents, fathers travel a lot, stressed, traffic, lonely, pri-

vate, no sidewalks, no front porches, malls, busy, materi-
alistic, quiet, pretty. I found the list poignant, with its mix
of dreams and disillusionment. Given this, I said to the
group, is it any wonder that you have tensions in the
church? People don't check all this anxiety at the door
when they come to worship. They bring this environment
and all it represents with them into the mix of what they
want, expect, and hope from their church.

Finally, the group offered images of the church,
something from nature or technology that would provide a
symbol of what the church is like. An oasis, someone said.
A quiet lake, said another. Then came a voice, "We are like
an old, old oak tree. We have roots deep in this community
going back 150 years. We have new green leaves today as
the community grows. And we want to branch out into
new ministries for people." The church indeed still owned
the country crossroads sanctuary built in the mid-1800s
about a mile down the road. The oak tree image began to
take on life. They had found something that said who they
were both at this moment and over time. Something came
together that evening in a time of *kairos*. The tree is now
the church logo on all their stationery and publications
and the theme for raising capital funds.

This congregation had a strong sense of time as
progress and achievement in a competitive culture. They
had all the statistics and goals. But they needed still to
attend to a reading of what time it was based on the particular traditions, traits, and gifts of that congregation. It
was time to discern the deeper character and meaning of
life together in that place, and see how God might want
to write new chapters of an old story through those who
people the place now.

I think it is a telling fact that in the English language—the language of Western commercial culture and
material progress—we do not have a particular word for
kairos. We have no single term for the concept of time ful-

filled or decisive time, except to talk it out as I have been doing. I know some people who try words like "kairotic" to describe crucial moments, but that just does not work for me. We have to face the fact that our culture often overlooks this dimension of reality.

To consider *kairos* turns the accustomed world upside down, inverting the usual assumptions. I take it that this is what Jesus meant when he said, "The time *[kairos]* is fulfilled . . . repent *[metanoiete]* and believe in the good news" (Mark 1:15). "Repent" just doesn't seem to me the right English word for *metanoiete*. The Greek means more like a revolution, an overturning, a dramatic change of mind. Only with such a transformed mind is discernment of God's reality possible. "Be transformed by the renewing of your minds," Paul wrote to the Christians at Rome (12:2). "Let the same mind be in you that was in Christ Jesus," he wrote to Philippi (Phil. 2:5).

Getting to this new mind is truly grace. Discernment can only be received as gift. We can try to prepare for it through disciplined attention. But to see the world in a whole new way can only be a gift of the God who is making all things new.

Reflections

The Space of Our Lives

In earlier reflections I have referred to spatial dimensions of congregational life, including physical space as well as the circles of "social space" that congregations create. I want now to be even more concrete in considering space as a formative perspective in our daily lives and a constitutive dimension of our congregations.

Last summer I was asked to change offices. I found this traumatic. I had been in the same space for ten years in a building that serves mainly as the university chapel with only a few faculty located there. From the parking deck it was quite a hike up the hill to the chapel and then up to the second floor; I calculated it as a climb to the sixth floor of a building. But I liked the sense of elevation. My office was dark, to be sure, with one small window looking into the dense green of a holly tree. The room was the last on a dead-end hallway and was dominated by a concrete girder running lengthwise, giving part of the space a low-ceilinged hushing effect. The carpet was gray, the walls painted a gray-white. I had grown to like this odd place; it seemed monastic, both contemplative and severe. I worked hard in the quiet and found laughter or conversation coming from the hallway extremely annoying.

I moved across the courtyard to the main classroom and office building of the School of Theology. The new office has three tall windows with southern and western exposures, requiring me to keep the blinds partially closed against the sunshine most of the time. Two of the windows are just at or below ground level and open onto an enormous steampipe wrapped in silver insulation that runs through a well along the front of the building. The third has an open view of trees and shrubs and people climbing the staircase to the courtyard above me. The carpet is a bright blue-green, the walls painted white with a hint of blue. It's a lively space, part of a suite with lots of activity. I work with a hum of voices in the background and both the steampipe and the staircase to remind me of the constant pressures of university busyness.

I needed several months to adjust to this change. I even walked into the wrong building on some mornings, my memory framing a door at the end of a hallway. I can't really say which office is more productive for me, yet the space has made an enormous difference in what I imagine and anticipate for each day. The productivity question is foremost in the dominant culture (and many studies have been conducted on workplace environments and worker efficiency). But the space itself is foremost for me. I have had to make it my own.

The unique history of North America and its development predominantly by people of European heritage has produced three primary, often contradictory or paradoxical, perspectives on space. The first, of course, is the perception that space is open. Most Americans like to believe that space is unlimited, that there is always someplace else to go if you don't like where you are. We watch movies filmed in Western states with broad plains, soaring mountains, and an open sky. The main characters in our films—especially "action" movies—rarely seem to have mothers and fathers, sisters or brothers, or any of the other ties of covenant and responsibility that most of us know in our daily lives.

Wallace Stegner, chronicler of the American West, pegged this outlook well. The "culture of opportunity and abundance," he wrote, "has, up to now, urged motion on [Americans] as a form of virtue." "Adventurous, restless, seeking, asocial or antisocial, the displaced American persists by the million long after the frontier has vanished. He exists to some extent in all of us, the inevitable by-product of our history: the New World transient." Indeed, for Americans whose ancestors came here by choice and not in chains of slavery, much of the attraction was open space. Away from the tightly winding streets of European villages, the surrounding land fenced and controlled by laws of nobility and inheritance, immigrants could breathe freely and make their own way. Even now something like one-fourth of Americans change residence in any given calendar year.

Today, of course, most Americans live in cities.

Less than 2 percent make their living from a farm or ranch, working in the open air. But open space continues as a national obsession. The Atlanta metro area now has an estimated 1.5 million pickups and sports utility vehicles (SUVs), with bigger models rolling out of auto plants every year. Pickups evoke the rural life, with a large part of the chassis literally an open space. SUVs create a space for their drivers, not only by keeping other vehicles farther away, but by towering over many of them. They have huge interior spaces. Ads for them are filmed in the West, and depict (with eye-popping special effects) the vehicles' interior opening out into mountains and streams. They are built to climb mountain roads, even though virtually all their mileage will be accumulated in traffic jams trying to get to Home Depot for a bag of mulch.

The more Americans value open space, the more valuable it becomes. Ironically, space is a scarce commodity, bought and sold in the "open" market. This second perception is hardly new, though the vastness of North America encouraged the myth of unlimited space for several generations. European settlers from the beginning came looking for land. Often they had never seen the land they "bought." Instead they perused maps depicting not only natural features such as rivers and mountains, but also a grid devised by mechanical survey of the land without regard to its contours. They viewed the land from "above" in the abstract before they attempted to inhabit it. They bought lots and parcels from "developers" and marked off their property with surveyors' pins.

Manasseh Cutler, a New England Congregationalist minister who helped organize settlement of the Ohio Valley, wrote a promotional brochure in 1787 that exemplified the European outlook.

> The lands that feed the various streams . . . which fall
> into the Ohio . . . are interspersed with all the variety

of soil which conduces to pleasantness of situation, and lays the foundation for the wealth of an agricultural and manufacturing people. . . . The prevailing growth of timber and the more useful trees are maple or sugar-tree, sycamore, black and white mulberry, black and white walnut, butternut, chestnut, white, black, Spanish, and chestnut oaks [he names eighteen more varieties]. . . . Springs of excellent water abound in every part of this territory . . . actually interspersed, as if by art, that there be no deficiency in any of the conveniences of life.

Cutler was convinced that this land was the fulfillment of prophetic vision, that God was providing this new Eden for Christian civilization.

The myth of open spaces depended, too, on ignoring the civilizations already in place. European settlers needed to understand the Native Americans as less than human or otherwise without civil rights in order to justify pushing them out to "open up" more space. In Cutler's words, "Here we behold a country vast in extent . . . lately the dreary abode of savage barbarity." Many "Indians" (a European misnomer created by a spatial error) were forced into specific parcels set aside as "reservations," spaces reserved for them where they were to learn a new framework of time as productivity and space as property. When tribes have found ways to make their reserved land itself a productive commodity (with oil or casinos), European Americans have been chagrined; "reservations" were intended to be worthless spaces, encouraging "Indians" to leave them and join the "mainstream" of American society.

The economics of scarcity shape our cities today more than ever. Space is perceived to be a scarce commodity. Prices for housing space in Atlanta have gone crazy in the last few years. I call it the backwash effect. Land speculators and developers have platted subdivisions fifty miles out from Five Points, the city "center." Now as those 1.5 million pickups and SUVs join the other nearly 2 million autos and trucks on metro area roads, many people want to live closer in. This has made space in the city ever more precious, measured, of course, in price per square foot. This drives out the people who can't afford such prices.

Congregations are caught up in the same dynamics, of course. They compete with other organizations for adequate land, favorable zoning, and visible, accessible locations. They acquire more lots for parking and find themselves leveling ridges and cutting down trees while wrestling with their consciences over their stewardship of God's creation. They need to build where the people are, even when the people are participating in the urban sprawl that so often diminishes the very quality of life and natural environment that attracted settlement in the first place.

Scarcity of space leads directly to the third perspective. We experience space as bounded, with the boundaries getting higher and more fortified all the time. Crowded together, we work harder to protect our personal space. The emerging urban life includes neighborhood patrols, gated "communities" with armed guards, and razor wire fences around parking lots and warehouses. We have invisible boundaries as well, marking off our spaces through clothing styles, language, and skin color. We know where we "belong" and we do not usually go where we do not "belong." It is not our kind of space.

Thus our experience of space is increasingly as compressed as our experience of time. Our myth of mobility—open space to go anywhere—is essential to the master myth of progress. But we also realize that what geographer David Harvey called "time-space compression" is pushing us closer together and forcing our lives into an interdependence unprecedented in global history. Even as we know we need to cooperate in order to make the city work, we are ever more rabid in protecting our personal space and privacy, and ever more enraged at drivers, cashiers, or public workers who get in our way.

Computers and telecommunications have compressed spaces of interaction in another way, to the point of making space seem irrelevant. With the Internet I have far more communication with friends in Europe than with many of my colleagues down the hall in the same building. In fact, most of our school memos are sent by email now, with the same spatial relationship to me as "outside" messages have.

I have traveled to Europe four times in the last five years. It's still a long distance; I still get homesick after ten days; significant differences in language, money, beds, and toilets all remind me that I'm not at home sweet home. Yet I can hardly find a souvenir to bring home that I could not purchase with less trouble at a local store. Some Christmas ornaments I picked out last year were labeled "made in China." Window-shopping in Warsaw shows me Barbie dolls and Nike shoes, McDonald's cheeseburgers and Robert Schuller paperbacks translated into Polish.

But if geographic space and distance seem to make less difference anymore, our own spaces of home and well-being still matter deeply to us. This is true wherever we are in the world, and just as much at church as at home.

Reflections

Reveries of Space

A couple of years ago I decided to contact a realtor and start looking for a house. I had been living in apartments for a while, most recently a complex (which is just the right word for these human anthills) populated mostly by twenty-somethings. I like Springsteen and even a little Metallica now and then; but when it comes through the walls from another apartment, no. I had grown weary of being able to hear my neighbor sneeze, but I found even more disruptive the daily arrival of rental trucks for people moving in or out. I felt as if I had a suite in a roadside motel. The night I was jarred from deep sleep by a drunk driver laying rubber through the parking lot and crashing into someone's parked car, I decided to call ReMax.

Most of all, I wanted my own space. I wanted, as the title of Michael Pollan's book had it, "a place of my own," a space on which I could put my personal stamp. I longed for the solitude of a space where I could find both haven and quiet, where I could make a home and create a room just for writing. The possibilities of such a place, to borrow Pollan's words, "began to occupy my imaginings with a mounting insistence."

Jim and George the real estate agents had seen my type before, I'm sure, though on an aggravation scale of one to ten I probably ranked somewhere around eight. I was committed to finding a house in this neighborhood, but the first fifty of them registered barely a blip on my interest radar. I discovered that the realtors were learning about me, though; they were watching and listening carefully as I looked at one space after another. When he brought me to the house I did indeed buy, George announced that "you're really going to like this place." The lot was a swamp of red mud; the building had a roof and walls but no windows or doors as yet. But I knew right away that George had me pegged. It was going to be the right place. Then my realtor turned theologian; it was "providential," Jim said, that this house was still available (the other five new houses on my block had sold). With that, I signed on the dotted line.

What they learned about my sense of space probably could not be written down. I could list such things as high ceilings, an open feeling, lots of big windows, a logical floor plan, a site below street level with a sense of a private cove. But really it is all those factors and many others added together into some intangible compound that stirred me to buy.

Jim and George could not have known one critical element in that compound, which was my memories of other houses. I looked at one house that was startlingly similar to the house my maternal grandfather lived in for sixty-seven years. I liked the lot and the screened porch and the way you could see from the front door right through to the kitchen, but after returning to it twice (George waiting patiently) I still saw it as Pop's place more than mine. I needed a space in harmony with my memories of houses in which I felt at home; I also needed to embody those values in a space of my own.

Such memories of spaces form a significant range of human imagination. Gaston Bachelard was one of few philosophers to explore in depth what he called "topoanalysis"—the meaning of places *(topoi)* in our lives. In his intriguing book *The Poetics of Space* he probed the content of human reverie or daydreams, often using the Greek term (anglicized in translation) "oneirism." In reverie, "Memory and imagination remain associated, each one working for their mutual deepening. . . . Through dreams, the various dwelling-places in our lives co-penetrate and retain the treasures of former days." All of us, he argued, have oneiric houses to which we return for a sense of home. We all retain "images of *felicitous space* . . . the space we love" (which he called "topophilia"). We need this imaginative world because "our soul is an abode. And by remembering 'houses' and 'rooms,' we learn to 'abide' within ourselves . . . the house is one of the greatest powers of integration for the thoughts, memories and dreams of mankind." Bachelard then took his readers on a tour of the house, showing how memories of a garret with a view, a cellar in cool darkness, a hearth in the center, even a drawer in a chest full of items I've collected, can become images that nurture my sense of wholeness and continuity.

Bachelard has been severely criticized for failing to acknowledge either his own class assumptions about houses—typified by his native France, of course—or the nightmarish rooms of memory retained by people who grew up in situations of poverty or abuse. Yet I find his analysis compelling nonetheless. A habitable space is one in which I can comfortably daydream. Conversely, my reveries weave a fabric of images in which I feel at home in the world. This is an imaginative task, a labor of love, exhausting when I tour rooms of manipulation or spite, nourishing when I tour rooms in which my soul has been fed.

I often return in reverie to the house my Aunt Neeny has lived in for more than fifty years. For me it is a childhood house; I have been there all too little in my adult years. Her house was the site of many family reunions over the years, but I don't think that's why I daydream about it. I think I go there in reverie because it so enriched my imagination with its variety and mystery. The house had so many kinds of spaces: two sleeping porches, a master bedroom large enough to hold a dance, what I used to think was the world's biggest bathroom with doors opening into three different adjoining rooms, a kitchen and breakfast nook with windows all around, a spacious living room and dining room with high, open-beamed ceilings. Best of all, the house had an attic spread out under the eaves, so vast that as a little boy I would stand at the bottom of the stairs leading to it and gaze up in awe (or maybe that was because my big sister used to tell me to stay out, that it was her space).

And I would stand looking down into the cellar, cool stone, shelves lined with the biggest model train I'd ever seen, and a shower right there in the corner of the concrete floor.

Could the brown shingle siding of Aunt Neeny's house have something to do with my house in Atlanta having an accent of brown shingle siding on its front garret? Why do I display the engine and coal car of my childhood model train on the sofa table in my living room? What is compelling about these images but their way of making my life whole through time and space, weaving my wildly disparate experiences into a single fabric of memory and imagination? This is my soul's work.

For wholeness I need both bright vista of garret and dim damp of cellar, both fresh air of front porch and warm coals of hearth. In Pollan's view, the genius of America's quintessential home-builders (of the Anglo male variety)—Henry David Thoreau and Frank Lloyd Wright—lay in their balance of centripetal and centrifugal, inside and outside. They wanted their houses to have both the hearth on which to curl up and an openness to the surrounding woods. Wright achieved this with glass; Thoreau, with less access to technology, just built very thin walls. Having stood on the site of Thoreau's cabin in Concord and visited some of Wright's houses, I remember what they were trying to achieve, and those memories, too, become part of my striving for balance.

This work of the soul in seeking wholeness is a deeply religious impulse. Our faith that things hold together, that the varied experiences and challenges of our lives are "bound together" (religio) with integrity, is central to our religious practices. One of those practices that intrigues me is the way we make spaces in which to be "church," a community of faith.

When I moved to Atlanta ten years ago, the

same principles of househunting came into play as I looked for a local church congregation. I just could not get comfortable in the standard Southern Protestant red-brick building with a high, white-frame steeple and temple columns across the front. The plain white paint of typical sanctuaries, combined with clear-glass Palladian windows, prominent wooden pulpits, and red carpet just made me so restless I could hardly sit through the service. I had to find a space with the resonance of my spiritual home.

I was encouraged in pondering my images of church by Hopewell's chapter in *Congregation* titled "househunting." I have always wished he had explored this metaphor more thoroughly. He did argue that a church building, like a house, is a kind of dwelling, and that studies of churches use methods similar to the ways people look for a house. He suggested four primary approaches to househunting. One looks first at the context or situation of the house (church), its surrounding neighborhood, main streets, accessible institutions, and distance from other important places in one's daily life. Second, one examines the mechanics of the house, its basic systems for heating, cooling, water, and power. The househunter is interested, third, in the floor plan of the house, the flow of movement and communication among rooms. Finally and more elusively, one seeks a fit between one's identity and what the house symbolizes, the image it projects and the values it expresses. Hopewell then identified the literature on churches that uses each of these respective approaches. All four, he argued, are necessary to understand a church.

One might extend the metaphor usefully in several directions. Pastor and theologian Carlyle Marney used to point out that people are drawn to different parts of the house that is church. People have varied gifts and outlooks that make them feel at home in certain spaces. The tinkerers and fixers (usually men) love the cellar with its dank furnace room and rusting hot-water tank. The extroverts who never meet a stranger like the front porch, where they can shake hands with newcomers and show them into the house. Folks who want the church to be just like home spend a lot of time in the kitchen preparing meals. The more introspective people of prayer gravitate to the upper rooms. Some people like the rooms with soft chairs where they can just talk. Some prefer the more spartan spaces with hard tables and chairs where they can study together. And the kids have the run of the place, looking for the space where they will be most at home.

My oneiric church building, the religious space of many of my reveries, is the building of Grace Church in St. Louis where I grew up. On the corner of a main thoroughfare three blocks from Forest Park, site of the 1904 World's Fair, the zoo, and several other St. Louis institutions, Grace always seemed to me to be at the epicenter of urban life. I liked arriving at the tall, stone structure with its red-tile roof, and the way the heavy wooden doors swung shut against the traffic noise outside. Climbing a few steps up to the sanctuary doors gave me a sense of elevation, of a place set apart. The sanctuary itself was a marvel for a little boy. The arches soared overhead, and I could not keep my eyes off the figures of the frieze in the proscenium arch—angels soaring toward a lovely Mary with child. The south rose window broke the sunlight into hundreds of brilliant jewel tones. The dark wood of the pews gently curving to form a semicircle facing the platform, and the general dimness (there never were enough light fixtures), added to the focused hush of the congregation.

Is it merely coincidental that the church building in which I decided to worship in Atlanta is three blocks from Grant Park, site of the Atlanta zoo, or that it has curved wooden pews facing a central pulpit, with colorful stained-glass windows in its south wall? I have no doubt that my reveries shaped my sense of space and particularly the space in which I could find a spiritual home.

Space, like time, is a reality most often taken for granted in American culture. Few people talk openly about the spaces of church, and the subject seems to come up mainly when architects get involved in a renovation or a new building. Yet I am convinced with Bachelard that space is the substance of reverie for the people who gather in our sanctuaries.

One of the most fascinating exercises I've ever conducted is what I call the "space walk." Our Candler research team designed this in 1988 when we were examining the relationship of congregations and public life in Atlanta. In each of the three churches we were studying, we invited a group of a dozen lay members to meet us on a Sunday afternoon at the church. We asked them to join us in a silent walk through the church building with long pauses in each of seven significant spaces. At those points we asked them to write on a pad of paper their memories, feelings, stories, colors, smells, sounds, or images of that space. We wanted them to attend to what architecture critic Tony Hiss called "simultaneous perception" as all their senses were in play at the same time, giving them messages about the qualities of a space.

We were astonished at the depth of reverie and meaning evoked by what might seem to be ordinary spaces of a church. At St. Luke's Episcopal, for example, the long, narrow nave with central aisle draws one's eyes to a mural high above the altar. There at the focal point of the sanctuary is a painting of Jesus as a beardless, boyish, Anglo-looking figure walking out of a mountain canyon toward the viewer, one sheep over his shoulder and others around his feet. He is holding a staff; he is draped in a loose-fitting cloth robe of Roman style; doves are in flight around his head.

One participant in our space walk, a man in his sixties, wrote on his pad that he had been baptized as an infant, had married, given away children in marriage, and witnessed the baptism of his grandchildren, at this altar under this mural. It was a source of comfort too profound for words. But whenever he looked at it even now, he remembered how as a little boy he would sit intently staring and trying to count accurately the number of doves fluttering in the background.

In the narthex at the back of the sanctuary, the group noted on their pads that the space seemed chilly and narrow. Tables were placed haphazardly against various walls with literature scattered on them. Old umbrellas and scraps of paper punctuated the corners. It was a space, they wrote, to pass through quickly from the street to the warm colors and sounds of the sanctuary.

The parish hall proved to be the most complex and thus most engaging space. It was the site of many of the congregation's activities, from adult church school and fellowship to a daily sandwich lunch served to more than four hundred homeless people. The day we walked through, the room reeked with disinfectant from a thorough mopping, a signal of one way in which the lingering presence of street people was wiped away each day. Yet in the middle of the room on a round table with white linen cloth stood a vase of long-stem roses giving off a sweet and elegant odor signaling a wedding reception. The linoleum floor was almost worn through from use, yet an elegant French provincial buffet and ornate mirror decorated one corner. The custodian's radio was sitting against a wall, piping the sounds of Roberta Flack singing "Killing Me Softly with His Song." At the same time one could also hear the chords of Handel's *Messiah* reverberating from the sanctuary pipe organ.

One person wrote that this was the real sanctuary of the church, a place for coffee, cigarettes, conversation, and community. Another called it "the World Congress Center" of the neighborhood (referring to Atlanta's main convention and exhibit hall), a place where all kinds of people meet, greet, and eat. Yet another noted that events just seemed to evaporate in this room, as one activity gave way to the next.

Discussing these reflections and reveries as a group of "space walkers," we agreed that we were touching on normally unspoken regions of meaning. We were expressing what usually lies outside articulation yet can stir deeply within us: our sense of space and its significance in our religious lives. Our space walk was a stroll through the "inscape" of the congregation, to borrow a term from the poet Gerard Manley Hopkins. He used the term to describe the pattern or design inherent in whatever he observed that he was trying to evoke in a poem. I expand it to name the interior terrain of image, memory, and feeling evoked by the spaces of the congregation and the accumulation of events and associations there over time.

If this region of sense has so much richness and depth, then, why do we explore it so little as individuals or congregations? I think this has much to do with the dominant commercial culture in which we live. Faith in the openness of space in America is inseparable from "freedom of religion" as we have practiced it. That is, we believe there is plenty of room for every religious group to make its own spaces and to leave one place and go to another if it so desires. On the other hand, if space is also a scarce commodity, its value lies not in meaning but in marketability. If space is a parcel to be fenced and protected, its significance as territorial domain for the like-minded overshadows its nature as a field for imaginative play.

These ironies were most apparent to me at the

side entrance to the St. Luke's building, which at the time was the main entry to the counseling center and church office. The doors were half timber, half glass. The glass portion was "protected" by a wrought-iron security grating shaped as a cross with beams of "light" radiating out from it. This double message of open arms of a cross defending an interior space was emblematic of conflict in the church over how its spaces should be used. It may also serve as a larger symbol of the tension between open and closed, available and commodified space in American culture. Further, it signifies that our understanding of space is a profoundly theological issue.

Christians are called to ministry in the real spaces of the world. If the gospel is to be redemptive it has to be incarnate in the spaces where people live in all their ambiguity and paradox. Yet it's also true that we expect a congregation to be a space apart. For many churches the sanctuary is a holy space marked off by elevation from the street, a high ceiling arching toward the heavens, and a hush of stone and stained glass. The liturgy is a kind of drama enacting the story of God's salvation, transporting the participants into a space of forgiveness, reconciliation, and joy. A lot of us want a worship service to evoke the awe of our faith, to bring us into the presence of the Holy One who is both absolutely present and absolutely absent in the spaces we create.

We also want our congregations to be spaces in which to grow in our ability to see and enact signs of God's reign in the world. As Saliers put it, "Worship in a particular space prepares us for God's presence in all others." Not that we are trying to create holy buildings that in themselves provide some guarantee of God's availability. But in "the beauty of holiness" we worship in order to join "the movement of life with God such that every time and place is touched with the fire of holy love and mercy."

That brings my thoughts finally to Paul Tillich's insight that presence comes at the intersection of time and space. Where time and space are in balance, we know presence. Only with a balanced hermeneutic of time and space can human beings enjoy presence and wholeness of life. Presence is inseparable, then, from *kairos*, for it marks the moment of fit when a particular time and space are appropriate for each other. At that moment, specific space expands to astonishing capaciousness and time opens on eternity.

I used to hope for such moments of presence every time I conducted worship, even knowing full well that the most I could expect was maybe once in five Sundays. The congregation would gather from many places in the city, bringing with them all the distractions of daily life. Sunday morning was the only time most of them saw one another, so the chat before the service began was always lively. Even an organ prelude and opening hymn rarely got the full attention of everyone there, and when the children's sermon came along the pandemonium threatened any liturgical flow that might have begun.

But then, at times I could never predict, perhaps during a prayer or an anthem, maybe just a certain verse of a hymn, or even in a sentence of a sermon, the space of the sanctuary would perfectly meet the time of our worship. And we would become a congregation. At some time out of time, in this space out of space, we would leave time as commodity and space as private parcel and become one body in the presence of each other and of the Holy One.

If I knew how to package that sort of *kairos* or provide the ten steps to fullness of space, I would write that instead of these letters and reflections. All I know is that it just happens. We make our spaces in the hope that presence will visit us. And sometimes, even here, it comes, a sign of grace and hope.

Reflections

A Sense of Place

Time and space constitute the everyday world of assumptions in which we live. The two dimensions are distinguishable yet inseparable, and it is their convergence to which I now turn. One name for this convergence is the sense of place, a sense that is palpable but often assumed and unspoken in congregational life.

Recent years have brought a growing and widespread interest in the sense of place. A whole scholarly literature examines how authors of novels communicate the place in which their narrative is situated and out of which it grows. People interested in regional cultures often write about the unique sense of place that distinguishes, say, Appalachian coves, coastal islands in the Carolinas, or the "Northeast Kingdom" of Vermont. A new generation of urban planners is concentrating on the mix of architecture, density, traffic flows, and uses that give neighborhoods a feeling of wholeness. And throughout American history town builders have attempted to create places of well-being—utopias—that combine features of the "ideal" life. The question of what makes a place "ideal" leads right back to the complex, elusive, but intriguing concept of a sense of place.

A scholar of American folklore named Barbara Allen suggested four elements that compose a sense of place. First is nature; place is geographic, a particular area of land with its distinctive geological features, climate, vegetation, and animal life. Much of the sense of "what kind of place this is" derives from whether the land is forested, arid, wetland, elevated, or sea level; whether the winter endures for six months of snow, browns, and grays, or the summer brings six months of hot, humid air and downpours of rain; whether a walk in the countryside brings sights of pelicans and flamingos, or of beavers and moose.

Nature shapes the uses to which humans can put the land, which is the second factor in the sense of place. Much of the character of mountain regions from Appalachia to the Rockies derives from the mining industries that have left their scars there. Harbor towns are known for streets winding along the shore and the snapping noise of mast lines on sailboats tied up in the marinas. New York's Manhattan is a massive outcropping of granite that supports the most astonishing collection of high-rise buildings in the world. Pittsburgh, Louisville, St. Louis, and Memphis are among many cities built along rivers and shaped by both the commercial traffic of ships and barges and the ebbs and flows of the waters.

Third, over time the human use of the natural place develops a lore of tales and wisdom that constitutes a history of shared experiences. Anyone moving to Atlanta hears the story of Sherman's march to the sea in 1864, even though his army's burning of most structures of what was then a small settlement can hardly hold a candle to the destruction of buildings and neighborhoods through highway construction and speculative development over the last fifty years. A visit to Boston is not complete without a stop at Old North Church or some part of Paul Revere's ride. If you pass through Brainerd, Minnesota, you have to get a photo of Paul Bunyan standing tall above the prairie.

Thus, fourth, a sense of place is consciously articulated, elaborated, and conserved. The features of nature, human use, and history combine to make a distinct identity of which inhabitants are aware. Even if the residents do not much discuss the place or what it means to them, a proposal to cut down a historic oak tree to widen a road, or to build a skyscraper that throws a shadow across a whole block of adjoining buildings, will quickly bring out the qualities of a place that people are ready to defend.

A sense of place does not belong exclusively to historic preservation or tourism. People often speak as if "real places" are only those somehow set apart, domains of quaint interest outside and protected from the maelstrom of daily activity. A visit to a "real place" is something we save for vacations or "get-away" weekends. But every place has a unique sense about it, particular features that give it a distinctive character. The task is to bring those features to articulation so that we can reflect more consciously and constructively about what kind of places we inhabit.

The conclusion that "real places" lie somewhere else does convey an important truth, though. The sense of place takes a constant battering from the commercial culture in which we live. If time is always only productivity and progress, if space is bounded commodity traded on the "open" market, if nature is the passive and inert resource for human projects, then a sense of place cannot flourish. Henri Lefebvre in his book on the production of space was among the first to call for ways to prevent "abstract space from taking over the whole planet and papering over all differences." Human character and distinctiveness, the particularities that give life substance and meaning, belong to places in which nature and human use collaborate over time to produce an identity.

Commercial culture brings with it what James Howard Kunstler called "the geography of nowhere." This generic landscape is replicated in all American towns and cities; it is especially evident along interstate highway interchanges or roads leading to them. As geographer Anne Knowles put it,

> The geography of nowhere . . . encourages consumption by making public spaces inhospitable to human interaction. It creates the illusion that it doesn't matter where we live and work, because one place is

pretty much like another. It fosters neglect and ignorance by separating the workplace from the home
and segregating people by class and race.

Even the "restoration" projects in older cities, intended to
foster an image of unique traditions, come out looking
pretty much the same. Union Station in St. Louis has
much the same ambience as Harbor Place in Baltimore,
not just because the same developer "restored" both of
them but because there is in place a dominant commercial image of what such "places" ought to look like, the
kind of people they should attract, and the sort of business and residential development that should cluster
around them. Forbes Field in Pittsburgh, Sportsman's
Park in St. Louis, and Municipal Stadium in Kansas City
have all fallen to the wrecking ball. Today's architects of
baseball parks replicate the features of these fallen monu-
ments, but Jacobs Field in Cleveland and Coors Field in
Denver come out somehow the same. When Atlanta
jumped on the bandwagon a few years ago to build
Turner Field as an "old-fashioned ballpark," it came out
handsome but looking ridiculous in its setting, echoing
the brick and piping of old northern industrial cities on a
site with few surrounding structures and a neighborhood
of white-frame southern bungalows. It's a great stadium
for watching baseball, but as a structure it has the feel of
being just one more commodity.

The dynamics that produce the geography of
nowhere have been in place for a long time, certainly
throughout American history. Much of it derives from
the expectation of mobility and freedom, which in turn
has depended on the myth of free, open, and available
land. As Wallace Stegner put it, "Nothing in our history
has bound us to a plot of ground." We have made a virtue
of moving on or up, always with the expectation of finding new amenities and comforts. Ironically, our constant,

restless movement has eventuated in a commercial landscape that is stifling in its sameness. We lose our grip on
what makes a real place. Stegner eloquently detailed the
attributes of place:

> A place is not a place until people have been born in
> it, have grown up in it, lived in it, known it, died in
> it—have both experienced and shaped it, as individu-
> als, families, neighborhoods, and communities, over
> more than one generation . . . it is made a place only by
> slow accrual, like a coral reef. . . . No place is a place
> until things that have happened in it are remembered
> in history, ballads, yarns, legends, or monuments . . .
> no place is a place until it has had a poet.

To grasp what makes a place itself, to name its distinctive
qualities, is a task of poetics. Naming the memories and
images associated with place, we call to mind the fullness
of a place's meaning. A place nurtures imagination and
thereby feeds our souls.

To be in a place is to know where you are, and
to know where you are, in Wendell Berry's words, is to
know who you are. The fullness of our sense of place is
inseparable from our sense of well-being and wholeness,
proportionality and justice, to which the scriptures continually point us. These themes resonate through the lives
of congregations that both embody a sense of place and
are poised to be among its most vocal advocates.

Reflections

Abiding in a Place

The sense of place brings us directly to the
dynamics of congregational culture and to questions of

how to appreciate, respond to, and lead that culture. The struggles of American society to achieve some sense of balance between continued economic development and the soul's longing for place are vividly played out in congregational life. Congregations also hold the possibility of enlivening and enhancing the sense of place for themselves and for their communities.

Some years ago Wade Clark Roof devised a very useful distinction between Locals and Cosmopolitans. In any community and any church one may find Locals, whose families have lived in that place for generations, who retain and retell the local customs and myths, and who view with distance and even suspicion those who would alter their ways. Cosmopolitans are those who have lived in other places, see the relativity of local ways, and take an interest in variety and diversity.

When Locals and Cosmopolitans mingle in the membership of a local church congregation, their clashing worldviews can produce some spectacular—and dangerous—fireworks. Usually this mirrors what is going on in the surrounding community. As Atlanta expands into fifteen counties, economic development has swept into and over many historically small towns. Main Street, the Chatterbox Cafe, and Vern's Groceries were once the meeting places for Locals who had known one another's families for generations. Now if they are not run out of business by Cracker Barrel and Publix, they survive as one more commodity. "Local history" is an image to be marketed to people buying houses in the new subdivisions who want "small town" values without actually living in one.

Meanwhile back in the congregation, the Locals know that the new Cosmopolitans are not part of the traditional fabric of relationships and are not committed to preserving local ways. When the Cosmopolitan newcomer comes to the church council meeting to urge selling the old campmeeting grounds to a developer and using the income to build a family life center, all hell breaks loose. And if the seminary-graduate pastor has put that Cosmopolitan on the church council, his or her pastoral tenure may be limited.

Such distinctions can be distorting if over-drawn, of course. Few people are either wholly Local or wholly Cosmopolitan. Most are a mix and the typology is useful only to help clarify the mix, not to polarize it. Few people are either only rooted or only uprooted. Most are a blend of connectedness with traditions and places and new attachments and relationships. To pose local culture and cosmopolitan change as opposites creates a false choice. The challenge is to nurture a vital culture that embodies the best values of both older and newer ways.

In his essay "Of Dwelling and Wayfaring," Erazim Koha'k showed how images of the ploughman and the wayfarer run through much Western literature. The former dwells in a place, tills the land, makes a home. The latter travels light, seeks the open road, and never really arrives anywhere. Koha'k warned against polarizing these two metaphors of human need. Both dwelling and wayfaring, incarnation and freedom, belong to the human soul. One cannot be subordinated to the other. Each needs the other. We are all a blend of the two (and more).

Koha'k's middle image to supersede the threat of polarity was the metaphor of pilgrim. "The pilgrim's basic posture is one of dwelling, of reaching out to the land and all the particularity of incarnation in love and labor, yet with the wayfarer's awareness that that home can find only transient instantiations on this earth." The pilgrim makes a home wherever his journey leads him, and carries the image of all those homes wherever he is. The pilgrim both incarnates life in a particular place and expresses the freedom of life in knowing that home is not permanent.

The pilgrim is an appealing image with deep resonance in a nation of immigrants. While immigrant Americans have always been on the move, they have also always been trying to make a home. While we worship the open road, we also need a place to which to return. In the cadences of biblical faith, the pilgrim is always journeying to new points of understanding even while continuing ancient practices, always seeking to appropriate the faith in his or her own life while being drawn into the incarnations of faith in the life of continuing communities. I think of the story of Abraham and Sarah as emblematic of this double movement. They follow the call of God to "go from your country . . . to the land that I will show you," and when they arrive they build an altar at the oak of Moreh, giving it the name Beth-el, house of the Lord (Genesis 12). They journey; then they make a place.

The sense of place recalls us to that balance where time, space, and natural environment meet holistically in our lives. Thus the sense of place is indeed a protest against the ruthless uprooting of peoples and the destruction of the past, characteristic of colonial wars and unbridled economic development. On the other hand, the sense of place gives no justification for narrowness and bigotry that purports to defend "us" and "our neighborhood" against a "them" that is too often people of another ethnicity or economic class.

If I decry "the geography of nowhere" and the commodification of places, it is only because I believe that the accelerating logic of capitalism does indeed, in Harvey's words, create "instability in the spatial and temporal principles around which social life might be organized." Economic development, technological invention, and ever more compressing time and space do indeed throw our lives and communities out of balance. We need a strong countervailing perspective.

Scott Russell Sanders compellingly appealed for a restored sense of place. By "staying put," he argued, we can learn to be true inhabitants of the places we have been given to live. "The understanding of how to dwell in a place arises out of a sustained conversation between people and land." To the extent that this bears fruit in a greater harmony of time, space, and nature, our habitation will help in healing the earth. It will also bring healthier communities.

Dwelling in a place is not a parochial act; this is one of the shrewdest lies of commercial culture. In Sanders' words, "All there is to see can be seen from anywhere in the universe, if you know how to look." But you must be somewhere in order to look, to pay attention, and to learn how to be an inhabitant. "How can you value other places if you do not have one of your own? If you are not yourself placed, then you wander the world like a sightseer, a collector of sensations, with no gauge for measuring what you see. Local knowledge is the grounding for global knowledge." "By learning how to abide in a place," we can learn the qualities that make for a healthy and just community. And by making a healthy and just community, we can join in the work of making a healthy and just world.

The more I have observed local church congregations, the more I am convinced that they are uniquely situated to be advocates of a sense of place. They are gathering places of pilgrims, repositories of local lore and also proponents of a world-embracing faith. Some people might argue that contributing to healthy and just communities is not the churches' primary task, that they should not get distracted from the essential goal of saving peoples' souls. But a holistic sense of place is profoundly spiritual.

Sanders put it this way: "If we are ever going to dwell in the house of the Lord, I believe, we do so now. If any house is divinely made, it is this one here, this great whirling mansion of planets and stars." Thus we must learn well what it means to make a place. Few of us, he continued, "imagine that the condition of our souls has anything to do with the condition of our neighborhoods." But if we cannot dwell where we are, then what could be our hope for the world? "I cannot have a spiritual center without having a geographical one," Sanders concluded. "I cannot live a grounded life without being grounded in a place." Although I am a little reluctant to accept the absolutes of Sanders' declaration, he certainly got my attention. I hear a lot of people talk about how much "spiritual hunger" they see in our society. I think—with Berry, Sanders, and many others—that this is profoundly a hunger for place.

A sense of place is in our bones wherever we live, work, and worship. The task is to attend to it and nurture it, in order to enhance the well-being and justice of our communities and world. Churches that worship a God incarnate who loves the whole world can surely find ways to advance this vital sense.

A Congregation in a Place

August 14

Dear Ken,

As I write to you this morning and imagine you
and your congregation, I immediately picture the slender
white steeple of your church building rising above the
lakes and hills of Grand Rapids. I remember how that
steeple is visible from many different roads, but one vista
in particular comes to mind now. Only the top of the
tower appears above the forest in this view, and it is not
immediately apparent how one would get there from this
standpoint. No telling from here what kind of church it
is; even that clever little sailing ship weathervane can't be
picked out in sufficient detail from here, though I know
it's there.

You know how a path curving away out of
sight through the woods draws you to walk along it with
far more zest and curiosity than a straight sidewalk
marching out in front of you as far as the eye can see. In
the same way I'm more attracted to the steeple for not
immediately knowing how to get there from here. As I

learn the streets that traverse the forest (meaning, of course, your town), I imagine more clearly how to get there, and those imaginings are the map of my sense of that place.

All was forest once. Sometimes when I'm walking the woods of your region I think I hear footfalls, as if ancient peoples were slipping past these trees on the way to trap fish in the lakes or to watch with me as the sun sets over the cold, still water. I know it probably wasn't these present trees, of course, because the European settlers logged over 90 percent of the land in just fifty years. Farming and logging became the main industries, at least until Henry Ford started building cars. Then vacation tourism caught on with factory workers and city dwellers seeking escape to the lakeshore as a change of pace and "return to nature."

I remember how hard it was for you and your family to get used to living there after moving from a much larger city with more cultural diversity. The built landscape was certainly different; the daily vista as you drove to work or school was unfamiliar. Even though you had vacationed in Michigan many times, it took some time to identify with it as the place you inhabit.

This is a singularly difficult adjustment for anyone. I try to imagine, then, a whole population settling in an unfamiliar place. This has been the experience of all immigrants to America, whatever their land of origin. In the case of my own family, the successive migrations from Germany to Virginia to Illinois to Kansas spanned four generations. So in a relatively short time, hardly a breath by the historical sensibilities of Africa, Asia, or Europe, and less than the blink of an eye by the timescale embedded in the land, settlers have had to make a place. For many the adjustments were overwhelming; many people became suicidal or ill; many died or fled back to their homeland. For migrants in the ethnic minority,

making a place was a struggle against even stronger powers of prejudice that left them with the least inhabitable
sites.

No wonder we are such restless people. The
experience of uprooting and migration is still fresh for us.
I remember hearing stories of my grandparents and
great-grandparents rolling westward in covered wagons
toward Kansas. To me, riding my bike down a tree-shaded
street in Topeka lined with two-story houses of solemn
red brick and our own white frame home, such wander-
ings were as remote as the ancient Goths. Only later have
I learned, with Carl Jung, that

> I am under the influence of things or questions which
> were left incomplete and unanswered by my parents
> and grandparents and more distant ancestors. . . . It
> has always seemed to me that I had to answer ques-
> tions which fate had posed to my forefathers, and
> which had not yet been answered, or as if I had to
> complete, or perhaps continue, things which previous
> ages had left unfinished.

In your congregation you honor the story of the
New England pilgrims and their search for religious freedom in a new land. I would press that identity-bearing
myth further to note how deeply the whole experience of
migration—of uprooting and displacement, new rooting
and replacement—is etched in the very grain of most
American congregations. Constant movement with all its
attendant hopes and sufferings is signified in many
assumptions and practices, certainly in Protestant congregational life. The endemic restlessness in the immigrant soul lives on: there is never enough, there must be a
better place or a better way. We can never do enough to
satisfy our appetites for experience, novelty, and plenty.
We demand from our leaders constantly new ideas, new

anecdotes, new plans, new directions for our individual and collective "journeys."

Meanwhile we tend to take Lot's wife as parable and refuse to look back. We not only ignore, but often do not want to learn, the history of our life together in a place. We do not want to think about how our worldview rode roughshod over the peoples already dwelling in the land when our ancestors arrived. We take for granted our ways of inhabiting and let our notions of church and community go unexamined. Both congregations and pastors pay an awful price for this willful ignorance. "It is impossible to exaggerate," wrote Kathleen Norris, "how much the unconscious, the hidden story, dictates behavior" in families and, by extension, in the congregations where they gather. So the unaware pastor or leader wakes up "one morning to find that all of the unresolved conflicts of lo these many generations have just been laid at your door."

A continually onward-looking or forward-looking freedom is not, then, the whole story of our lives. In fact, we do have histories. We make places and seek our identities and hopes in them. We inhabit houses and make them home. We build churches in which we expect generations to seek the Lord.

The sense of place is a complex chemistry of nature, human use, history, and identification. It evokes the varied needs of the human soul for well-being. People identify with places, as geographer Anne Buttimer put it, in a reciprocal movement of "home and horizons of reach." Like breathing in and breathing out (my metaphor for ecclesiology as well), human beings need both home place and outward horizon, "rest and movement, territory and range, security and adventure, housekeeping and husbandry, community building and social organization." When these reciprocal movements are in harmony, one finds centeredness or coherence in a place.

"One's sense of place is a function of how well it provides a center for one's life interests."

A member of St. Luke's Episcopal Church expressed this dynamic eloquently in her notes from the "space walk" I wrote about earlier. Standing in the hallway just outside the south chancel door to the sanctuary, this woman, a regular choir member, noted the tension and exhilaration she associated with that space. The pipe organ would be playing, the service was about to begin, there was energy, warmth, chosenness, unity. There was also in the wall to the left of the door "the cold of a window pane . . . a window to the street below—a view of the world." Even as she was anticipating "a time to look inside myself" in the sanctuary, she could not help viewing the skyline of Atlanta's downtown as emblem of the world.

Congregations seem to me to be uniquely situated to explore and deepen this holistic sense of place in their communities. In many ways they embody, symbolize, and enact that double movement of home and horizon, incarnation and freedom. For one thing, they are places in which people deliberately seek the sacred. "Sacred space," wrote historian Belden Lane, "always possesses a double impulse—a movement which is at once centripetal and centrifugal, a pulling in and pushing out from a center, a tendency alternately toward localization and universalization." Congregations are thoroughly local, their buildings often constructed or accented with natural materials of the region, their people drawn from the area, their activities indigenous to the community. At the same time, their sacred text as well as their ritual and programmatic actions partake of a symbolism more broadly practiced in many times and places. Approaching the Holy in their own uniquely incarnated way, congregations also acknowledge that by definition the Holy exceeds their forms and any others.

A second way in which congregations express Buttimer's reciprocity of breathing in and breathing out is through their constant double movement of assembling and dispersing. They erect facilities, raise money, and offer varieties of programs for participants. Yet much of their stated organizational purpose occurs in dispersed form as members live and work in their community. So congregations exist most visibly when assembled, yet their identity would be incomplete without their disassembling to interact with the community of which they are a part.

Over time a congregation's place accrues, like Stegner's coral reef—the colors, textures, and endurance of memory and story. "The sacred place is the place rich in story," as Lane put it. Metaphors, images, anecdotes, tales, fables, even sagas and epics are woven around a congregation's symbolic objects and gathering places. Thus, third, congregations relate past and present in ways significant both to their own and their communities' histories. Around them are spun webs of meaning drawn from strands of personal journey, organizational event, community change, and larger faith traditions, that give both church and community a surer sense of self.

Finally, congregations are continually altering and deepening the sense of place as they repeat their practices of assembling and dispersing, remembering and acting. Congregations often serve as unique spaces in their communities within which public discourse about what people value can be sustained. They are spaces in which the qualities of life particular to a place are reflected and reinforced, yet also places which, because of their universal referent, offer some "horizon of reach" toward a critical perspective on local ways.

St. Luke's sits on Peachtree Street, Atlanta's most favored business address, just north of the downtown business district. The congregation's sense of place as it has evolved over the past century has been both a mirror of a changing region and a catalyst for justice in a city with enormous disparities of wealth and poverty. In the early part of the century the church exemplified what I call a landscape of classical progressivism. In 1906, St. Luke's moved from a downtown corner to what was then a street of Victorian homes. The congregation built a Gothic Revival English chapel with a long nave, narrow side aisles, and a wide central aisle paved with red tile leading one's eye to the high altar set against the far chancel wall. I have already described to you the mural above that altar. It was not only significant to worshipers; the mural was also one of Atlanta's first great pieces of public art. Commissioned in 1912, the painting was created by Edwin H. Blashfield, a muralist best known for his work in the dome of the Library of Congress. He belonged to the American Renaissance movement in painting, drawing heavily on classical designs and ideas.

The installation of the mural in 1913 was an important artistic event in Atlanta. The city was booming with a population of nearly 150,000, a 60 percent increase in one decade. Yet it was still a young town, and patronage for the arts was minimal. For a congregation to spend $3,000 on a work of art in 1913 Atlanta was remarkable. But a number of prominent women, including the wife of Georgia's governor, became involved in the project, collecting donations, selling aprons, and serving a businessman's lunch every day in a storefront near the church.

The rector in those first years on Peachtree was also a highly visible public figure in the city. Cary Breckinridge Wilmer wrote an irenic column each week for the *Atlanta Constitution*. In 1906 he joined with an interracial group of pastors to call for an end to race riots whipped up by angry whites. He was an outspoken opponent of journalist Tom Watson, whose racial demagoguery was wreaking havoc in Georgia. Again in 1915, Wilmer pleaded for a commuted sentence for Leo Frank, a Jewish man convicted of a child's murder in a case infamous for its lack of evidence, and Wilmer publicly deplored Frank's lynching at the hands of the Klan.

At the same time, Wilmer was deeply engaged as parish priest in the task of decorating the newly completed St. Luke's sanctuary. Over the ensuing twenty years he designed the stained-glass windows to depict episodes in the life of Christ, and supported the Blashfield mural project. In Buttimer's terms, Wilmer was shaping both the congregation's home space as well as its horizon of reach into public space, seeing them as complementary.

The outlook that gave coherence or centering to Wilmer's world was a moderate Christian progressivism intent on preserving the values of the European past — classical murals, Gothic stained-glass windows — while espousing a broad humanitarian concern for the suffering created by social and economic change. Yet in retrospect, his and the congregation's world seems very settled. Everyone had a place. Public order was based on authority of office or inheritance of power through an influential family. Social status could be measured, it was said, by "a pew at St. Luke's and membership in the Piedmont Driving Club."

A look into the life of St. Luke's at the end of the century brings out a very different landscape, now of diversity and transitoriness. The sheer growth of Atlanta had the greatest impact. From a mid-sized, compact city of 150,000 when St. Luke's was built, Atlanta has boomed into a metropolitan area of nearly 3.5 million people in fifteen counties. The Victorian homes long ago gave way to office towers and apartment buildings. Atlanta's central expressway cuts under Peachtree Street right next door to the church building, creating a vast "moat" of asphalt ten lanes in each direction, sunken below street level, carrying tens of thousands of people each day right past the church but without any relationship to that particular place.

The congregation reflected this exponential change in population and diversity. An older group of longtime members loyal to Episcopalianism was still very much bound to St. Luke's by family and social allegiances. But a large, second group was newer to the membership, younger, more educated, more mobile, and more professional in employment, half of them lacking any family or friendship tie to the congregation. Most of the latter group were attracted by St. Luke's public image of commitment to the city as symbolized by the soup kitchen.

A walk through the St. Luke's neighborhood vividly symbolizes the challenge of its sense of place. Like many cities, downtown Atlanta has been busily creating a two-story universe. Newer buildings typically encompass what architects call an "atrium," an air-conditioned indoor ecosystem of human invention and control, with glass elevators rising to the balconies of upper stories and green plants festooning the railings. Many of the buildings are connected by "skywalks," another grandiose developers' cachet, enabling people to pass from one atrium to another without ever going outdoors. Thus an executive in one of these buildings can drive in from the suburbs, park in an underground garage, work, eat lunch, meet for appointments, go to the car to drive home, and never set foot on street or sidewalk.

Meanwhile on the street under the skywalks, outside the atrium lobbies, people are waiting for buses, walking, sleeping in doorways, or asking for money. This is Atlanta's lower-level cosmos in which many people have no job and no place to go. In the upper story, people are at home in the land. The streets by contrast are transient, noisy, leading through neighborhoods of abandonment and desolation.

St. Luke's owns a lot of property around the church building. Their stewardship confronts them with vivid questions of what they can do to shape the sense of place for themselves and for their neighborhood, to reconcile the two-story universe of the city, and to tell and enact Jesus' story of reconciliation. One step was to create a lovely park along the expressway with trees, benches, and artwork for the public to enjoy. Another was to offer a soup kitchen and other social services for homeless people.

The sense of place is palpable at St. Luke's. Parishioners continue to be deeply attached even as the city continues to move through tumultuous change. The faith that they can make a healthy difference is inseparable from their habit of gathering in this certain place generation after generation. They can be a catalyst for a more fertile sense of place in the city as well.

American culture does not usually encourage a sense of place, but it seems to me critical to our future. The era of time and progress, expansion and exhaustion of earth's resources has to give way to greater balance. As art critic John Berger put it, "Prophecy now involves a geographical rather than historical projection; it is space not time that hides consequences from us."

I am encouraged to see more and more discussion of what we can do to seek this balance, where time, space, and nature meet to create the presence of a sense of place. Daniel Kemmis, the mayor of Missoula, Montana, argued that "what makes a good city is not its capacity to distract, but the way in which it creates presence . . . [making] it possible for humans to be fully present—to themselves, to one another, and to their surroundings." He and his fellow mayor Kurt Schmoke of Baltimore spoke of cities in "grace . . . a way of acting in the world which is strikingly appropriate to the time and place." They suggested that if people experienced this grace more often in their communities, they would be drawn to help construct a renewed public life.

Grace and presence are the native tongue of the church. With their habit of assembling regularly in a particular community, local church congregations have the possibility of nurturing and extending a sense of place. Together they seek those moments of *kairos* that can only be received as a gift, when time and space meet and congregants can be truly present with one another and with God. Gathering in spaces of symbol and memory, dispersing to everyday lives of work and play, breathing in and breathing out, congregations can be catalysts of grace and presence not only for their participants but for their communities. This is a deeper justice that goes beyond economic opportunity and tolerance of diversity, to the creating of a shared well-being and trust so essential to healthy human community. Surely, Ken, this presents a worthy calling for the church.

Tom

Concluding Reflections:
On Working with
Congregational Culture

Reflections

Learning a Congregation's Culture

Every congregation is a unique culture comprising the artifacts, practices, values, outlooks, symbols, stories, language, ritual, and collective character that make it particularly itself. This culture is an outgrowth of the life together of a particular mix of individuals, families, and ethnic and community forms that have connected in a certain place over time. By carefully observing congregational culture, leaders and participants can deepen understanding and appreciation for the congregation as it has endured. They can also realize what Denham Grierson called the "openings for ministry" made possible by building upon the congregation's values and strengths.

For pastors in particular, and also for lay leaders, learning the local culture is imperative for effective leadership. People do not accept a leader who does not know them well and demonstrate appreciation and love for them and their ways. They are much more likely to accept new people and new approaches if they have a sense of how the new continues certain values sustained in the past. They look forward to who they can become as a congregation if they are confident that their story has been heard and will be honored.

Moreover the congregation as a whole is deepened and strengthened by exploring congregational culture together. The learnings are not just functional leadership "tools," but shared discoveries that strengthen loyalty to the congregation as it seeks constructive change. The congregation is freed from the passive-aggressive "expert" model of being told what "works" and can enter into self-discovery of its own considerable gifts and strengths for ministry.

Congregational study further opens the way for congregations more explicitly to become communities of theological reflection. Participants can see more clearly how they are living out the claims of their faith, or how certain forms limit their witness. They can discover what Lewis Mudge called the "sacramental character" of their life together; their culture is revealed as an outward and visible sign or parable of ways in which an inward and spiritual grace moves through their life and work together. They can see their own lived theology and learn what Robert Schreiter called the "local theology" through which they live out collectively what they trust to be true about God and God's world.

I want to describe briefly an approach to learning congregational culture. Books such as *Studying Congregations* offer lots of detailed methods that are very helpful in organizing a study. Here I present a useful pattern that has emerged in my own work with congregations. I bring together participant observation, narrative, interviews, planned walks, and open-ended "brainstorming" questions, in a flow that leads from more thorough knowledge of congregational culture to constructive plans for extending the congregation's witness and service.

The first step is conscious and attentive participant observation, which is both a specific activity and an attitude that overlays all the other methods. It is the explicit activity that carries out what I called earlier an "ethnographic disposition." When I observe as a participant, I sit in worship services or church meetings and watch carefully. I make notes as unobtrusively as possible, often writing on a worship bulletin or meeting handout (a notebook can be conspicuous). I just try to record what happens: who is interacting with whom? Who plays the music and how does it sound? How do people walk forward for communion and how do they look? Where do people sit? What are the symbolic objects and how do people relate to them? What language or idiom is used in the meeting? Later I type those notes into my computer, which is the best way I have to digest what I've observed, recall incidents I forgot to make note of, and compare this event with other activities.

Participant observation is also an attitude. It begins with the question, What do these people think they're doing? If I were coming in from the other side of the world, what would I make of this activity? In other words, I'm trying to jolt myself out of the taken-for-granted aura of familiar hymns and creeds, the customs of handshakes and "how are you?" I'm trying to see things as if for the first time, resisting my impulse to assimilate.

Second, I try to learn the congregation's story, attending to the varied functions of narrative that I summarized earlier from Hopewell's work. Certainly reading histories and looking at documents and photographs is one means. I'm one of many people who have found it useful also to conduct a memory time line with participants. Anywhere from a dozen to twenty-five people representing various age and interest groups sit in a semicircle facing a long wall. Along the wall I have posted a sheet of butcher paper or newsprint perhaps twenty feet long. I draw a line the length of the paper about a third of the way down from the top. Above that line I will write what people remember of community and world events, and below it the congregation's stories.

I begin by asking participants, When did you become a member of this congregation and whom do you remember as among the first people you met here? I then write the first name of the participant and the year of membership on the time line, placing it proportionately between the church's founding date and the present. I use different-colored markers: blue for people's names, green for church programs mentioned, black for buildings, red for important events.

As the time line begins to unfold, I prompt discussion with questions such as, If you were to tell just one story that captures what this congregation is like, what story would you tell? What was going on in your neighborhood during those years? After everyone has had a chance to contribute and the time line is filling up (which usually takes about 70-80 minutes), I ask them to look at the story as a whole: What patterns do you see? What's left out? What have you learned that is new to you? I then ask them to speak single words or phrases that capture something that's true about the congregation; to name an image from nature or technology or some realm other than church that brings out the character of the congregation; and to suggest a biblical parable or image that is significant for this congregation. Finally, I draw the line a bit farther into the future, and ask what people anticipate and hope for as an extension of their narrative. When we're done I leave the paper on the wall for people to add to during other activities in the coming weeks.

This exercise has never let me down. People leave feeling affirmed and hopeful, even if some memories are painful and some stories are left untold. Newer members especially learn more about the congregation, but elder members almost always make discoveries, too. It's not unusual to hear someone say, "I've been a member here for years and I never knew that!" Best of all, the exercise shows how the narrative fabric of the congregation weaves together personal, corporate, contextual, and biblical stories to make a unique whole. People leave it with some ideas of what makes their congregation distinctive and the strengths it has upon which to build.

Interviews provide an important supplement to this collective exercise. Most pastors learn about their parishioners' lives through conversations in their homes or in hospital rooms; members learn about fellow members through social activities and classes. But few people can take time to construct an interview with thoughtful questions. Interviews can yield some amazing discoveries.

Hopewell had some poignant suggestions for interview questions: "Tell me about the way your faith has changed throughout the years." Or, "Think of the death of a friend or a relative. What do you suppose was going on?" To these questions, apt to evoke personal faith journeys, one adds queries about how the person experiences the congregation. "What changes have you noticed since you became a member?" Or, "At what points in the congregation's life do you feel closest to God . . . [or] in danger of losing touch with God?"

Such questions can evoke the deep connections of loyalty that bind people into communities of faith. They also bring out hurts that may never have been healed, and, unresolved, still reverberate in congregational decisions. In any case, they reveal the density of relationships and the tenacity of people's struggles to be part of a community that will offer companionship along the journey.

A similar depth of memory and meaning comes out in the "space walk" I described. I take a group silently through the building, stopping at each of perhaps eight different spaces — sanctuary, narthex, office corridor, Sunday school room, choir room, fellowship hall, parking lot, and others. We pause in each for five to seven minutes to write down memories and associations, to record feeling words, colors, sounds, and any reflections or reveries stirred by the space.

I've been amazed at how much a symbol such as a window, an altar rail, or a cross can mean to people, or how sensitive people are to changes of light and sound. This exercise, too, gets them thinking about their norms and expectations, and causes them to notice things (accumulated trash, cracked plaster, narrow doors) that they have been taking for granted as part of the landscape.

I like to conduct a similar walk out in the neighborhood. Arriving at the church building as most of us do in our two-ton cocoons of glass and steel, music thrumming on the stereo and climate control keeping us nicely insulated, we do not notice what the physical environment of the church building is really like. To get out and walk is to pay attention to vistas and sightlines, to hear and smell and see, to get the flavor of life in the neighborhood. This, too, can be supplemented with interviews, asking people on the street, in shops or offices what they sense going on in the area, how it has changed over the years, what kind of people they see here.

Some participants resist the idea of this exercise at first. They claim to know the area well enough already, or assert that no church member lives nearby anyway so what difference does it make. There's no place to walk, say members of churches at rural crossroads or suburban strip developments. But when they actually do walk, they are generally amazed at what they learn. The neighborhood has features—noise, vista, density, grace—that they may never have noticed. People previously unseen and unremarked are discovered nearby. Most of all, participants learn that even for a commuter church, its place is an essential feature of its identity and mission.

Last, I like to organize a day-long event involving a cross section of church leaders and participants with varying perspectives. I try to assemble people who are willing to look at things a little differently. In the room, preferably a retreat center or another building away from the congregation's facilities, I use all four walls to display what the congregation has learned about itself. On one I mount the memory time line as one version of the congregation's story, complete with key words and images that capture something of its continuing character. On another I post newsprint sheets that record sights, sounds, images, and reveries from the space walk inside and the neighborhood walk outside the church.

I spread several sheets of newsprint across tabletops, and write at the top of each sheet an open-ended question sparked by my own reflections on the preceding material. They all begin with the word "what," never "why." A "why" question puts people on the defensive, thinking they have to justify things. A "what" question forces them to make a positive suggestion. For example, I might ask, What can this congregation do to enhance the worship experience on Sunday morning? Or, In what ways can this congregation respond to the growing population of single adults in the neighborhood? Or, What can this congregation do to help people of different races get to know one another?

Like the space walk, this is a silent exercise so that people don't get into debates or commentary. I ask participants to circulate around, writing specific, do-able ideas on a sheet, then moving on to another. Gradually they begin to read other people's ideas as well, but I ask them not to comment on them (especially not to write, "We tried that before"), just let the other ideas spur their own thinking. When people have written what they think of, I post the sheets on the third wall.

That brings us to making specific plans. We sit surrounded by the congregation's story and character, the symbols and spaces of building and community, and a wealth of new ideas. We are immersed in both continuity and innovation. Now what should come next? Usually in small groups I ask people to begin ranking ideas, testing what stirs up their energy and imagination. These more fine-tuned ideas I post on the fourth wall and the group as a whole begins to decide what to work on, and what resources they can bring to these tasks.

I have found this method deeply affirming of the congregation. They do their own reflecting. They generate their own sense of their strengths, and discover their own "openings for ministry." The pastor and leaders learn much more about what drew people here in the first place and what keeps them coming back. They have a much more complete picture of who the people are and what they imagine for their life and work as a congregation.

Above all, people learn that they really are church. This very congregation has a vocation as a sign of what God's reign in the world is like. And God gives them the gifts of witness and service that they need to carry on Christ's ministries where they are.

Reflections

Crafts of Place

I am more than a little skittish about the possibility that thinking deeply about the culture of a congregation might become simply another program. "Our planning team proposes that this year's education emphasis will be to study our symbols. Then we will have Dr. Frank speak on time and space for our Lenten dinners." That's fine — I like speaking for church dinners — but that's not entirely what I have in mind.

I want simply and plainly to do whatever I can to help cultivate a certain disposition among people who have been set apart in various ways for leadership in the churches. I have called this an ethnographic disposition, by which I mean a disciplined way of observing the places and people among which we have a ministry. I don't mean that all leaders must be ethnographers per se, but I do hope that more would be drawn to what Clifford Geertz described as "crafts of place." By observing, describing, exploring, and working "by the light of local knowledge," leaders—particularly pastors coming from outside—have a much better chance of understanding their congregation and seeing the "openings for ministry" that will enable them to lead it.

I also want to appeal to pastors and lay leaders to make room for imagination in their work. In our reveries as persons and as congregations, we have the real possibility of discovering the images that stir us, that hold us close and bind us together. We can learn more clearly what life is really like for us in this congregation and in the community of which we are a part. Sharing our reveries, in conversation with imagery from scripture and church traditions, we can be both critical and constructive in pondering ways in which our congregation obstructs or continues the story of God's reign.

This is a poetic art, but again, I am not suggesting that all pastors or church officers be poets. I do hope that many will be drawn to practice the art of paying attention, of seeing the infinite in the moment. Hearing the sound of words, noticing "a pheasant disappearing in the brush," as Wallace Stevens said of poetry, the leader's imaginative world is alive and flourishing with insight.

Both the craft of ethnography and the art of poetry are "gratuitous" today, to use W. H. Auden's word. He was mourning the age when poetry had the power to define public life, as against today's societies of endless labor and consumption in which only productivity and acquisition are rewarded. But perhaps this gratuitousness is indeed a gift, as the word implies. To be able to see clearly, describe accurately, capture the telling image and the crucial detail, is properly a grace. Like all graces, like prayer, like consolation, the poetic gift must be received; but we can also cultivate our capacity to receive it.

Auden declared that if he had his way, students would be required to memorize poems, all books of literary criticism would be banned from the libraries, and anyone pursuing poetry would have "to look after a domestic animal and cultivate a garden plot." I note that both these latter mandates are work, to be sure, but in the end pure joy; or at least if they are not playful and joyful, I am going about them the wrong way.

So what can church leaders do, to extend Auden's second metaphor, to more wisely cultivate their gardens? What is the role of the tender and cultivator? I have implied a lot about this role in earlier reflections. Now I want to bring together the main themes more explicitly.

I think of five movements or rhythms, all interactive, each appropriate at a different moment. An essential aspect of these arts is to learn what is right for what time. First, of course, is observing. This is the discipline of watching, listening, noting, making connections, memorizing names and stories, attending to times and spaces. Observing is a shared activity, not the detached omniscient gaze, but the participant who is playing a special role of noticing things and talking with others about what he or she sees.

Second is affirming. Simply by learning the stories, the leader as cultivator is honoring the congregation as a storied community with its own integrity. Naming the strengths and resources he or she sees in the congregation, the leader affirms the gifts the whole body has for ministry. This may often be a moment of healing as well, since many stories reveal, hide, or sublimate past divisions and conflicts. To affirm is not to gloss over past hurts, but to name them for what they were and see if it is not possible now to move on. The act of naming may also provide a compelling image that, like a gyroscope or compass, becomes a continuing guide for the congregation in decisions about its ministries.

A third movement in cultivating a congregation's culture is placing it in a larger context. In this moment the leader is helping to define what is particular to this congregation and to show connections with the surrounding community and larger church traditions. Putting the local in conversation with a wider context — of neighborhood, society, and the witness of other churches — the leader is opening the way for the congregation both to appreciate its own uniqueness and see its own relativity.

This may be frightening or alienating for some participants, but the risk may also be just the right catalyst for enabling a congregation to give up hurtful or limiting patterns or for encouraging it to adopt new initiatives. For example, in a congregation many of whose members have moved away to other communities or suburbs, study of the sweeping patterns of migration in their region may be a source of encouragement that relieves them of guilt over "failed" ministry and frees them to see new possibilities in their situation.

Fourth, leaders have a key role in brokering cultures. I don't particularly like the market metaphor of broker in this context, but it does name something significant. Participants come into congregational life bearing many organizational cultures. They have been shaped by schools and places of work. They bring memories of other congregations. Their imaginations reel with the bombardment of media and advertising from commercial culture. Now they are trying to be part of this particular congregation's culture. Moreover, the whole congregation is struggling to imagine more deeply the society of well-being and justice that God envisions for the world.

Leaders help people make sense of these disparate cultures, the ways in which they collide and the means by which they can make a constructive fit. Taking the cultural materials at hand—the mill where many church members work, the tension between the old town and its new exurban subdivisions—leaders try to help people see how gospel may be at work in and through their congregation and its ministries. They also help people discover and claim language and images from the imaginative resources of a vital religious heritage that will enable them to live with integrity in the multiple, segmented cultures of their daily lives.

The fifth movement is generative—the poetic art, the moment of creating. Like a gardener trying a new arrangement of flowers or a new variety of tomato, the leader is inventing, playing with possibilities, inviting people to risk the uncertain based on what they already know. From the materials of symbol and story, leaders create new rituals and establish new patterns. They offer language for interpreting the congregation's situation. They pose words and images to evoke new energies and stir new hopes in the congregation.

In one case, a pastor might have the opportunity to help a lay committee design a ritual for moving from a historic sanctuary to a new building constructed next door. How will the symbols and spaces of the old be honored in the new? How can gestures—a procession of symbolic objects, a song of "marching to Zion"—provide lasting images of transition and making a new place? In another case, a lay leader might reflect upon a memory time line exercise showing the amazing story of rebirth in

a congregation once given up for dead and name her congregation "the butterfly church," connecting the image
with deeply held analogies to resurrection and new life.
In yet another case, a congregation might gather at the
burned-out shell of their beloved sanctuary, where their
leaders pulled the stone baptismal font from the ashes, set
it up as the focal point of their worship, and led everyone
in renewing their vows to be faithful in witness and service whatever may come. Through such imaginative acts,
church leaders become mentors and models for the creative expression of others.

One way to name the arts for which I'm plead-
ing might be this: church leaders can do a great service
just by asking their congregations to take a breath. A
deep breath can relieve us from constant striving, acting,
changing, serving, evangelizing, and being on a mission—relief from a constant breathing out but never in. If
we keep on exhaling, we reduce faith to activity, to action
that must have influence and exercise control. To breathe
in is to refresh, to receive, to attend to what we have been
given. It is to explore our heritage of symbol and story,
and to appreciate the gifts we have already received for
witness and service of God's reign.

I told you that I often ask people in a church
for a biblical image that captures something that's true
about their congregation. I've been amazed at how regularly the story of the "good Samaritan" comes up. Here is
a parable for people's highest hopes for themselves, an
image of what they would like to be and how they would
like to be perceived—helping people in need, being there
for people who suffer, giving of their resources to lift people over the rough spots.

I don't often let this one go by unremarked. I
like to point out that Jesus didn't call the Samaritan fellow "good"—he just described what he did. I take this to
mean that the Samaritan was an ordinary guy with all the

faults and failings the rest of us have, who happened to stop and help somebody else. He acted like a neighbor. So doing similar things won't make this congregation particularly "good," certainly not in the sense of removing its blemishes. But stopping by the road is still the right thing to do.

My other dig in the garden is to provoke people's imaginations. Who are you in this story? I ask. Almost all the time, the participants in this exercise imagine themselves as the Samaritan. They see themselves as among the blessed disciples, bearing the social assumption that "we" always have the resources to help "others" and are never among the needy (at least "we" shouldn't be). The only exception to this image that I distinctly recall came from an African American congregation in which people first of all remembered their times of need and how they had been helped. They imagined themselves initially as among those who had been battered and left by the road. Strengthened by that memory, they could identify with the hurts of others and be a neighbor to them.

To tend the garden well is to direct people's attention to their own brokenness. In their broken soil, they may be blessed with new shoots of green. The gardener is interested above all in the soul of the congregation, the character of its collective life, and the quality of its spirit. Here, where life is made out of the materials to hand, with all the ambiguities and failures accompanying our efforts, we learn who we are and who we can be in the presence of the Creator.

I wrote earlier about the cross at St. Luke's that forms a security grate over a side door. There is another cross, too. It is of a piece with the stone of the arch over the main Peachtree Street entrance. This cross has a jagged crack from top to bottom. It is a cross that has been lived, that has known some brokenness. But still it holds together and blesses all who enter there. Knowing that congregation and its ministries, I just can't imagine that I'm the only one who has noticed it.

Reflections

Imagining a New Creation

Some years ago I went on a tour to the "Holy Land" with a church group from Kansas City. We had expert leaders and congenial friendship, but on the whole, I would have preferred to travel incognito and explore the place for myself. For me just about anything would have been preferable to being stuck on a bus riding down the byways of the Middle East with thirty other white midwestern Methodists. One time I was strolling alone through the side streets of Jerusalem and a stranger approached me with the words, "Rabbi, can you tell me the way to the West Gate?" I was thrilled with a rush of identity and belonging. But then it was back to the bus.

Parked atop the Mount of Olives, our cameras clicking, we were swarmed by clusters of Palestinian boys selling fifty postcards for a dollar. Much to our chagrin, we were replicating the ugly spectacle of white Americans reaching for U.S. dollars and buying off people of color just to get them to go away. "This is terrible," muttered somebody in the travel group as we settled back into our seats, "all this commercializing of the Holy Land."

"Oy vey," I replied. "Get a grip. Can you imagine if Jesus had been born in Branson?" Things were very quiet on the bus for an hour or two.

But in fact I couldn't imagine Jesus being born in Branson; that's what made my tease, such as it was,

We were unmistakably in an ancient place, and there was something about the land itself that gave it the character of revelation. For such a small region it was marked by astonishing contrasts. Here was Mount Hebron rising four thousand feet above the valley; fifty miles away was the Dead Sea sinking well below sea level. Here were miles of desert wasteland, and suddenly an oasis of trees in the middle of nowhere. Here were rugged bluffs of Judean wilderness jutting out toward barren rocky hills; there were caverns opening down under the earth like rooms of a palace. No sooner did I conclude with one breath that "the land is like this," than I was balancing that with a contrary observation.

I can't help thinking that Jesus' gospel itself grew in some way out of this land, or that the irreconcilable contrasts of the place made fertile ground for Jesus' ironies. If the reign of God really does turn the world upside down—the last are first, the rich are poor, the prisoners are freed, and so on—what better place to imagine this than a land where nothing is the same from one mile to the next. The place is as full of paradoxes now as it was then.

After visiting there, I'm no longer surprised that most of the literature in the Bible was penned by people living in the caves, not the Temple. Prophecy was a child of the wilderness, not the settlements. It now seems sensible that Jesus grew up in Capernaum, not Jerusalem. Jesus preached mostly to the common village folk, not the ruling class. The ruins you see there today are mainly atop hills, where the powerful built their fortresses to control the roads. Which hills Jesus was on we don't know, because he was just walking by and left no ruins. Yet he is among the most remembered of all the land's inhabitants.

These paradoxes are fertile ground for revelation. They continually astonish me. So much the more so does the Incarnation itself. That God chooses to show what God is like through a human being is amazing enough. That God would do so in an anonymous village by a fishing lake near highways where competing armies have marched up and down for centuries boggles the mind. Yet the unexpected is the spring of imagination by which we, too, are able to incarnate signs of the reign of God.

Imagination is sparked by the juxtaposition of opposites, the collision of difference. A metaphor puts words from distinct conceptual worlds side-by-side to make new meaning (a "running argument," the "idea" that didn't "pan out"). Likewise images that stir us leap to life out of the unlikely and unanticipated bumping together of unassimilated realities. The same gospel that is obscure to me as I pour myself a cup of coffee in my kitchen and anxiously review my workaholic schedule for the day, is suddenly vivid to me when a woman sitting outside her hut in a Guatemalan village gestures to me — a stranger on a "mission" trip — to sit beside the road and have a cup of her hard-won coffee. Who is on a mission to whom? Gospel turns the world on its head.

Congregations are incarnate communities. In their breaks, paradoxes, conflicts, and differences revelation is born. We devote extraordinary amounts of energy to glossing over distinctions and inuring ourselves to surprise. We prefer routine to paying attention; we have our paths well-worn and cleared to avoid any stumbling blocks. How much we miss.

Among the Presbyterian churches in our recent congregational studies at Candler was a church I finally started calling Tory Dissenters Church. It was just so WASP, the parking lot full of Mercedes and Lexus, the people looking like models for Brooks Brothers. They had broken away from Anglicanism many generations ago; but they were still so very English.

I wasn't prepared by my stereotypes for my seatmate one Sunday, in a pew about ten rows from the front. This twenty-something woman, sitting alone on the aisle, was a photo from a women's wear catalog. But the liturgy moved her from one dimension to three. She opened her mouth to sing "Holy, Holy, Holy." She knew all the words to all the verses. From there we sailed on through the creed and the Gloria. She even recited the collect without looking. She left quickly after the benediction, before I could introduce myself. She left me to wonder about my types, labels, and reductions. Who am I to say what gospel means to her, or what I think it ought to mean? Wouldn't I have to ask her?

I would like her to meet Mama Gray, though. Actually I often have this fantasy that people I run into in various congregations ought to meet and talk together. I think of how much they could learn from one another, and how much joy they could take in the revelations of being together. I met Mama Gray in Boston in a United Methodist congregation that has more than thirty nationalities represented in its membership. She was African American, well up in years, and blind. She stood up in worship one Sunday during prayer concerns and said, "I have to tell you, you all look awful good to me this morning." "Look"? What could she mean? She was imagining everybody there; I mean, we were really there, but she had to imagine us. I have never felt more fully like a real creature of God than I did that morning.

So I figure that if Ms. Tory Dissenter who's got the whole liturgy memorized and Mama Gray who's got every person in the congregation in her mind's eye could meet and talk together, between them they would "have church" like nobody's ever seen. And maybe that's already going on within our congregations and we just haven't noticed the springs of imaginative life already flowing through our lives together. Imagination already in itself creates a space in which we have unlimited possibilities for empathizing with the lives and situations of others. This is the empathy on which Jesus drew, speaking parables to offer signs of God's reign of love and justice.

It pains me that our congregations so often replicate the divisions of our world. People of diverse ethnic groups and social classes usually do not meet through our churches. We see our differences as incommensurable and defend our worlds. Yet all our efforts to eliminate paradox are failures. Even homogeneity cannot prevent revelations in the breaks of our lives. A poetics of congregational life requires that we make room. We must make a space in our personal and collective lives to imagine, to remember, and to dream. No longer taking our world for granted, we have a chance to know that God doesn't either.

Little in our dominant culture of competition and consumption encourages us to explore the spaciousness of our lives. That culture can make us feel regimented by time, closed in anxious spaces of scarcity, alienated from our neighbors, and fearful of our future. Inevitably our congregations take on these qualities, too. At some points the literature about congregations even seems to encourage us to extend the anxious competition into church life.

The *kairos* is here to nurture the soul of the congregation. Congregations already have immense resources for imagination, plenteous gifts for witnessing and serving the reign of God. The dream that most captures me is a vision of church leaders, pastors and laity, taking time and making space for greater balance in their lives, so that they can explore the rooms of story, symbol, memory, and image that offer fullness of life for their personal and collective pilgrimage.

Someday I want to go back and visit the Mount

of Olives again. The Palestinian boy who sold me those postcards is probably almost thirty by now. But maybe he and his family, and Fayez our bus driver, and his wife and children, and what the heck, all those other white midwestern Methodists, could just sit up there awhile together. If we could just be together and tell the stories of our lives, the reign of God would seem very near. The people of Mayflower and St. Luke's and Big Bethel would show up, and soon we'd be feasting on barbecued chicken and some strong, hot coffee.

Jesus sat up there once, too. And someday, maybe when we're all together on the mountain, he'll sit there again.

Notes

Page | Reference

21   Thomas Reeves, *The Empty Church: The Suicide of Liberal Christianity* (New York: Free Press, 1996).

22-24   Thomas Moore, *The Care of the Soul: A Guide for Cultivating Depth and Sacredness in Everyday Life* (New York: HarperCollins, 1992), 214, 303.

24   Richard Nelson, *The Island Within* (New York: Vintage Books, 1989), 45.

33   *The Book of Discipline of The United Methodist Church 1996* (Nashville: United Methodist Publishing House, 1996), 114-15.

33   Susan Frank Parsons, unpublished paper on mission.

33 34   George Barna, *Marketing the Church* (Navpress, 1988), 21, 37. Norman Shawchuck, Philip Kotler, Bruce Wrenn, and Gustave Rath, *Marketing for Congregations* (Nashville: Abingdon Press, 1992), 47-48.

34   Meredith Willson, "May the Good Lord Bless and Keep You" (Milwaukee: Hal Leonard Publishing, 1950, 1981).

39   Emil Brunner, *The Misunderstanding of the Church* (Philadelphia: Westminster Press, 1953), 10, 11, 16-17.

40   Leonardo Boff, *Ecclesiogenesis: The Base Communities Reinvent the Church,* trans. Robert R. Barr (Maryknoll, N.Y.: Orbis Books, 1977, 1986).

40   James F. Hopewell, *Congregation: Stories and Structures* (Philadelphia: Fortress Press, 1987), 11.

43   John Vannorsdall, "The Boundaries of Our Habitation," *Weavings* 6/1 (January-February 1991): 25-28.

44-45   Pierre Bourdieu, *Outline of a Theory of Practice* (Cambridge: Cambridge University Press, 1972, 1977), 29-30.

47   Craig Dykstra and Dorothy C. Bass, "Times of Yearning, Practices of Faith," in Bass, ed., *Practicing Our Faith: A Way of Life for a Searching People* (San Francisco: Jossey-Bass, 1997), 7. Dykstra, "Reconceiving Practice" in Barbara G. Wheeler and Edward Farley, eds., *Shifting Boundaries: Contextual Approaches to the Structure of Theological Education* (Louisville: Westminster/John Knox Press, 1991), 50, 54.

48   Bourdieu, *Outline,* 79.

49   Hopewell, *Congregation,* 15.

50   Charles Wesley, "Jesus, United by Thy Grace," in *The United Methodist Hymnal* (Nashville: United Methodist Publishing House, 1989), 561.

50 "Move closer to each other," an image from Dorotheos of Gaza, quoted and discussed in Roberta C. Bondi, *To Love as God Loves: Conversations with the Early Church* (Philadelphia: Fortress Press, 1987), 25.

50 Frederick Buechner, *Telling the Truth: The Gospel as Tragedy, Comedy, and Fairy Tale* (New York: Harper and Row, 1977), 23.

52 Hans Küng, *The Church* (New York: Sheed and Ward, 1967), 84-86. For discussion of the emergence of *ekklē-sia* as a term, see Wayne A. Meeks, *The First Urban Christians: The Social World of the Apostle Paul* (New Haven: Yale University Press, 1983), 80, 108.

61 Jackson W. Carroll, Barbara G. Wheeler, David O. Aleshire, and Penny Long Marler, *Being There: Culture and Formation in Two Theological Schools* (New York: Oxford University Press, 1997).

62 Samuel Heilman, *Synagogue Life: A Study in Symbolic Interaction* (Chicago: University of Chicago Press, 1973, 1976), xi, xii; Melvin Williams, *Community in a Black Pentecostal Church: An Anthropological Study* (Prospect Heights, Ill.: Waveland Press, 1974), xi; Charles R. Foster and Theodore Brelsford, *We Are the Church Together: Cultural Diversity in Congregational Life* (Valley Forge, Pa.: Trinity Press International, 1996), 12.

63 Nancy Tatom Ammerman, *Bible Believers: Fundamentalists in the Modern World* (New Brunswick: Rutgers University Press, 1987), 12-13.

67-68 *Vital Congregations—Faithful Disciples: Vision for the Church,* Foundation Document of the Council of Bishops of The United Methodist Church, Thomas E. Frank, principal writer (Nashville: Graded Press, 1990), 17-18, 21.

70   Gaston Bachelard, *The Poetics of Space*, trans. Maria Jolas (Boston: Beacon Press, 1958, 1994), 39.

71   Paul Ricoeur, "The Metaphorical Process as Cognition, Imagination, and Feeling" in *On Metaphor*, ed. Sheldon Sacks (Chicago: University of Chicago Press, 1978, 1979), 151.

71-72   Bachelard, *Poetics*, 47.

72   Wallace Stevens, "A Collect of Philosophy," in *Collected Poetry and Prose* (Library of America, 1977), 851, 865.

72-73   Kathleen Norris, "Drawing on Metaphor," *Christian Century* 114 (September 24–October 1, 1997), 842.

74   Hopewell, *Congregation*, 16.

78-79   The dimensions of culture are defined by Joanne Martin, *Cultures in Organizations: Three Perspectives* (New York: Oxford University Press, 1992). Geertz's terminology is explored in Hopewell, *Congregation*, 55. See Clifford Geertz, *The Interpretation of Cultures* (New York: Basic Books, 1973), 6.

79-80   Hopewell, *Congregation*, 11.

81   The extended quotation is from my essay "Congregations and Theological Education and Research," *Theological Education* 33/2 (Spring 1997): 110.

81   The Hartford study was published in David A. Roozen, William McKinney, Jackson W. Carroll, *Varieties of Religious Experience: Mission in Public Life* (New York: Pilgrim Press, 1984); Carl S. Dudley and Sally A. Johnson, *Energizing the Congregation: Images That Shape Your Congregation's Ministry* (Louisville: Westminster/John Knox Press, 1993).

81-82   Denham Grierson, *Transforming a People of God* (Melbourne: Joint Board of Christian Education of Australia and New Zealand, 1984), 17.

83   Williams provides an exemplary analysis of seating patterns in *Community*, 144ff.

83   Grierson, *Transforming*, 43, 64.

89-90   Hopewell's three dimensions of narrative in congregational life, *Congregation*, 46-49.

90 91   The Korean church's words are quoted in *Vital Congregations*, 54.

91   Lewis Mudge, *The Sense of a People: Toward a Church for the Human Future* (Philadelphia: Trinity Press International, 1992), 109.

91-92   Foster and Brelsford, *Church Together*, 30-35.

93-94   Williams, *Community*, 86-88, 116.

95-96   Mudge, *Sense*, 4, 107.

96-98   Much of the description of Big Bethel is taken from Thomas E. Frank and James W. Fowler, "Living Toward Public Church: Three Congregations," unpublished paper (Atlanta: Candler School of Theology, 1990), 29, 51.

98   Hopewell, *Congregation*, 10, 15.

99   Mudge, *Sense*, 214.

105-6   Edward T. Hall, *The Dance of Life: The Other Dimension of Time* (Garden City, N.Y.: Anchor Press/Doubleday, 1983), 43-46.

109   Hall, *Dance*, 49.

112   Don E. Saliers, "Sanctifying Time, Place, and People: Rhythms of Worship and Spirituality," *Weavings* 2/5 (September-October 1987): 18-29. See also his book *Worship As Theology* (Nashville: Abingdon Press, 1994).

114-15   See article on *kairos* in Gerhard Friedrich, ed., *Theological Dictionary of the New Testament,* vol. V (Grand Rapids: Wm. B. Eerdmans Publishing Co., 1967), 455-62.

115   For discussion of *kairos* in rhetoric, see James L. Kinneavy, *"Kairos:* A Neglected Concept in Classical Rhetoric," in Jean Dietz Moss, *Rhetoric and Praxis: The Contribution of Classical Rhetoric to Practical Reasoning* (Washington, D.C.: Catholic University of America Press, 1986), 79-105.

121   Wallace Stegner, "The Sense of Place" in *Where the Bluebird Sings to the Lemonade Springs: Living and Writing in the West* (New York: Penguin Books, 1992), 199-206.

122-23   Manasseh Cutler, "An Explanation of the Map . . ." and "Sermon Preached at Campus Martius, Marietta, North-West Territory, August 24, 1788," in William Parker Cutler and Julia Perkins Cutler, *Life, Journals, and Correspondence of Rev. Manasseh Cutler, LL.D., by his Grandchildren,* vol. II (Cincinnati: Robert Clarke and Co., 1888), 397-98, 438-50.

124   David Harvey, *The Condition of Postmodernity* (Cambridge: Blackwell, 1990), 284.

126   Michael Pollan, *A Place of My Own: The Education of an Amateur Builder* (New York: Random House, 1997), 4.

127-28   Bachelard, *Poetics,* xxxv, 5-8.

129   On Thoreau and Wright, see Pollan, *Place*, 19-21.

132   Tony Hiss, *The Experience of Place* (New York: Alfred A. Knopf, 1990), chap. 1.

134   Gerard Manley Hopkins (1884–1889) used the term "inscape" liberally without definition, though some notes illuminate it; see Catherine Phillips, ed., *Gerard Manley Hopkins* (New York: Oxford University Press, 1986), 235. John Patton also discussed the term in *From Ministry to Theology: Pastoral Action and Reflection* (Nashville: Abingdon Press, 1990), 34, with a reference to Alfred Margulies, *The Empathic Imagination* (New York: W. W. Norton, 1989).

135   Saliers, "Sanctifying," 24-25.

136   Paul Tillich's reflection on time, space, and presence may be found in the collection of his writings entitled *On Art and Architecture,* ed. John Dillenberger and Jane Dillenberger (New York: Crossroad, 1987), 84-85.

137-38 Barbara Allen, "Regional Studies in American Folklore Scholarship," in Barbara Allen and Thomas J. Schlereth, eds., *Sense of Place: American Regional Cultures* (Lexington: University Press of Kentucky, 1990), 1-13.

139   Henri Lefebvre is quoted and discussed in Harvey, *Condition*, 237.

139   James Howard Kunstler, *The Geography of Nowhere: The Rise and Decline of America's Man-Made Landscape* (New York: Simon and Schuster, 1993). See also Michael Hough, *Out of Place: Restoring Identity to the Regional Landscape* (New Haven: Yale University Press, 1990).

139-40   Anne Knowles, "To Choose a Place," *The Other Side* (July-August 1994), 14-15.

140   On restoration projects, see Harvey, *Condition*, 295.

140-41   Stegner, "Place," 201-5.

141   Berry paraphrased in Stegner, "Place," 199.

142   Wade Clark Roof adopted this typology from Robert K. Merton and others, in *Community and Commitment: Religious Plausibility in a Liberal Protestant Church* (New York: Elsevier, 1978), chap. 3.

142   On marketing local history, see Harvey, *Condition*, 303. For an intriguing and in-depth study of transitions in a small-town, now exurban, congregation, see Nancy L. Eiesland, *A Particular Place: Urban Restructuring and Religious Ecology in a Southern Exurb* (New Brunswick, N.J.:Rutgers University Press, 2000).

143   Erazim Koha'k, "Of Dwelling and Wayfaring: A Quest for Metaphors," in Leroy S. Rouner, ed., *The Longing for Home* (Notre Dame: University of Notre Dame Press, 1996), 30-46.

144   On capitalism, see Harvey, *Condition*, 239.

145-46   Scott Russell Sanders, *Staying Put: Making a Home in a Restless World* (Boston: Beacon Press, 1993), 32, 114-17, 120, 121.

148   On the Michigan logging industry's belief in the "inexhaustible" forest, see Bruce Catton, *Waiting for the Morning Train* (Garden City, N.Y.: Doubleday, 1972).

149   C. G. Jung, "The Tower," in *Memories, Dreams,*

Reflections, ed. Aniela Jaffe (New York: Vintage Books, 1961, 1965), 223-37.

150   Kathleen Norris, *Dakota: A Spiritual Geography* (New York: Ticknor and Fields, 1993), 84.

150   Anne Buttimer, "Home, Reach, and the Sense of Place," in Anne Buttimer and David Seamon, eds., *The Human Experience of Space and Place* (New York: St. Martin's Press, 1980), 170-72.

151-52   Belden Lane, *Landscapes of the Sacred: Geography and Narrative in American Spirituality* (New York: Paulist Press, 1988), 19, 28.

152-56   Much of this material comes from Frank and Fowler, "Living Toward Public Church." In the years since our study was completed, St. Luke's has undertaken extensive renovation of its buildings and grounds.

156   John Berger, *The Look of Things* (New York: Viking Press, 1974), quoted in Edward W. Soja, *Postmodern Geographies: The Reassertion of Space in Critical Social Theory* (London: Verso, 1989), 22.

156   Daniel Kemmis, "Living Next to One Another" *Parabola* 18/4 (Winter 1993): 6-11. Kemmis quotes Schmoke.

161   Grierson, *Transforming,* 129, 167.

162   Mudge, *Sense,* 116.

162   Robert Schreiter, *Constructing Local Theologies* (Maryknoll, N.Y.: Orbis Books, 1985).

162   For methods of congregational study, see Nancy T. Ammerman, Jackson W. Carroll, Carl S. Dudley, and

William McKinney, eds., *Studying Congregations: A New Handbook* (Nashville: Abingdon Press, 1998). For exploring the history of a congregation, see James P. Wind, *Places of Worship* (Nashville: American Association for State and Local History, 1990).

165   Hopewell's provocative interview questions may be found in *Congregation*, 90-92, 143.

169   On "crafts of place," see Clifford Geertz, *Local Knowledge: Further Essays in Interpretive Anthropology* (New York: Basic Books, 1983), 167.

169   Wallace Stevens, "Adagia," in James Scully, ed., *Modern Poetics* (New York: McGraw-Hill, 1965), 150.

169-70 W. H. Auden, "The Poet and the City," in *Modern Poetics*, 167-82.

170-71 On the significance of naming congregational images, see Dudley and Johnson, *Energizing*, 91-93.

175   Some of this material was published as a sermon, "Creating a Space" *Pulpit Digest* 75/528 (July-August 1994): 43-47.

177   I'm grateful to my friend Weldon Durham for telling me the story of his cup of coffee on a mission trip to Central America.

178   Mama Gray is captured on film in the video accompanying the United Methodist Bishops' Initiative, "Vital Congregations—Faithful Disciples" (Nashville: United Methodist Communications, 1990).

179   On the empathic imagination, see Richard Kearney, *Poetics of Imagining* (HarperCollins Academic, 1991), 224-25.